IT MUST BE TRUE

IT MUST BE TRUE

CLASSIC NEWSPAPER HOWLERS, BLOOMERS AND MISPRINTS

DENYS PARSONS

ILLUSTRATED BY ANTON AND HARO

EBURY
PRESS

5 7 9 10 8 6

Copyright © 2002 Estate of Denys Parsons

First published 2002 by Ebury Press
An imprint of Random House
20 Vauxhall Bridge Road · London SW1V 2SA
www.randomhouse.co.uk

Random House Australia (Pty) Limited
20 Alfred Street · Milsons Point · Sydney
New South Wales 2061 · Australia

Random House New Zealand Limited
18 Poland Road · Glenfield · Auckland 10 · New Zealand

Random House South Africa (Pty) Limited
Endulini · 5a Jubilee Road · Parktown 2193 · South Africa

The Random House Group Limited Reg. No. 954009

Printed and bound in Great Britain by Bookmarque Ltd

A CIP catalogue record for this book is available
from the British Library.

Cover by Graham Rawle

ISBN 009188687 2

CONTENTS

INTRODUCTION

Denys Parsons compiled his first book of howlers *It Must Be True – It was all in the papers* in 1952, and didn't look back. Over the next four decades he published more than a dozen best-selling misprint volumes, each a true labour of love. His name fast became a byword for misprint humour. The book you hold in your hand, taking its name from Parsons' first volume, has gathered the best of these timeless howlers together for the very first time.

In his first book, Parsons claimed it was reading a passage from a cookery book that initially gave him the urge to start collecting misprints: "If it is a cold day, cut a few slices from your tongue and serve with brown sauce." A true howler enthusiast, on coming across an item, Parsons would sit back with closed eyes and relish visualising the scene: "The Churchillian jaw was out-thrust and the Prime Minister thumped the dispatch box with a heavy fish."

The mistakes on show are of several types: some are editorial misprints, the fault of tired sub-editors and copy-writers, where the wrong word is inserted; others feature innocent but unfortunate phrasing where the sentence is suddenly imbued with a whole new meaning; finally there are typesetting and compositor mistakes – and in the days of hot metal these mistakes in particular could take on an inspired insanity that would be hard to match today.

In addition to collecting these gaffs himself and receiving contributions from his readers, Parsons would trawl back issues of humorous magazines such as *Weekend*, *Punch* and *The New Yorker* to gather his quarry. All the misprints were, according to Parsons, one hundred per cent true. Although some, he felt, were perhaps the result of in-house mischief among bored sub-editors and typesetters. He tried to give the exact source of the publication wherever possible, but many magazines that quoted misprints would often omit the exact name of the original magazine or newspaper to save the blushes of the editors.

BIRTHS, DEATHS
& MARRIAGES

Students who marry during their course will not be permitted to remain in college. Further, students who are already married must either live with their husbands or make other arrangements with the dean.

Syllabus of an Ohio College

MR AND MRS JOHN NASH WILDING, OF 880 FIFTH AVENUE, ANNOUNCE THE ENGAGEMENT OF THEIR DEBATABLE DAUGHTER, MISS VIRGIN A. WILDING, TO MR LUIS MARCELLINO DE ACEVEDO OF BUENOS AIRES.

New York Tribune

Municipal Judge Charles S. Peery, who performed the brief wedding ceremony, said plaintively: 'I forgot to kill the bride. And I'm sorry."

Tarrytown News

The bride, who was given away by her father, wore a dress of white figured brocade with a trailing veil held in place by a coronet of pearls. She carried a bouquet of rose buds and goods vehicles, leaving free access to all private vehicles not built for more than seven passengers.

Atherstone News and Herald

SISTERS WED BROTHERS
HAVE BABIES SAME DAY

New York Herald Tribune

20-year friendship ends at Nashville altar

Nashville paper

In 1911 he worried Mrs Laura Little of Montgomery, Alabama. They have three children.

Philadelphia Inquirer

The bride's bouquet was pink rose buds, and heather Stephanotis. She was attacked by the Misses Louise Carlton, her niece, Fiona Danvers, Jennifer Burns and Angela Burns.

Crawley Advertiser

Dear Sirs,
I am getting married soon and would like to know what causes this to happen and if there is a way of preventing it.

Letter received by Kodak Ltd

Miss Edith Seymour Clark, daughter of Mrs Howard Gates Clark of 983 Park Lane, will be carried on the afternoon of April 21st to Mr John Jacob Gunther, of 46 East 81 Street, in Christ Church.

The World

Mr John McCutcheon is married to Susan Dart of New Orleans instead of going to Australia as he requested.

New Orleans paper

The bride was very upset when one of her little attendants accidentally stepped on her brain and tore it.

Kent Messenger

. . . the bride wore a Spanish influenced dress with high neck, and frills on the leaves . . . The dress which was gathered at the back fell gently to the floor.

Middlesex Advertiser and Gazette

Two priests, one of them the uncle of the bride, travelled from opposite ends of Miss Virginia Hinglass to Mr Bernard McInnes in Dublin yesterday.

Dublin Sunday Independent

We have the sad duty to inform you of the death of M. Giovanni, recalled to God by accident.

Paris-Normandie

Mr. and Mrs. Benny Croset announce the birth of a little son which arrived on the 5.15 last Thursday.

West Union (Oregon) People's Defender

Ensign and Mrs. William A. Clark have announced the girth of a son, Kenneth William, on Oct. 6th at Neenah, Wisconsin.

Montclair (New Jersey) Times

Mr. and Mrs. — of Duke Hill are the parents of any infant daughter born Thursday.

Illinois paper

MR. AND MRS. JOHN BOWLEY ARE
THE PARENTS OF THEIR CHILD, A
DAUGHTER, BORN AT WINDSOR
HOSPITAL ON AUGUST 15.

Vermont paper

Mr. and Mrs. John Beverlin are rejoicing over an eight-pound daughter, their sixth child since last Saturday.

Illinois paper

A son was born to Mr. and Mrs. William Kleintop, Leigh Avenue, during the past week. Congratulations, Pete!

Palmerston (Pennsylvania) Press

On Wednesday of last week, two children of William Pass, near New London, fell into a 20-foot well accidentally. Fortunately the well was dry and the youngsters fell on top of one another so that their fall was broken.

Oxford (Pennsylvania) News

The bride looked charming. She carried a bouquet of white roses and carnations and the bridegroom.

Local paper

Immediately after the ceremony the bride and bridegroom go into the vestry and sigh.

Answer to correspondent

The bride was attired in navy-blue georgette and hat to match, and carried a bouquet of roses and baby.

Iowa paper

The marriage took place at Salter's Road Methodist Church, Gosforth, today, of Miss Gwendoline Dodds, Gosforth, and Lieut. Frederick Dodds, of 6 Kensington Avenue, daughter of Mr. and Mrs. E. Robinson, R.N.F., son of Mrs. E. Robinson, of 42 Blackwell Lane, Robinson. The bride was Darlington, and the late Mr. attended by Mrs. E. K. Rawlins and the best man was Lieut. F. McCormack, R.N.F.

Northern paper

The happy pair then left for Scotland by car. The parents were numerous and costly.

Local paper

When Miss Dixie Janice Byram, daughter of Mr. and Mrs. R. C. Byram of this city, became the bride of Edward Hersey on Friday afternoon at 2 o'clock at many friends here occurred last overshirt of lace. Her hat was the First Presbyterian Church.

Winter Haven (Florida) Herald

One of the many engagements that are always announced at the close of the season if that of Miss Caroline Stackley.

The World

One of Colorado's oldest citizens and a resident of Walsenburg for almost a century died here yesterday. Mrs. Quintina was 104 years old at the time of her death, her grandmother said.

Brockton (Massachusetts) Enterprise-Times

The bride, who was given away by her father, wore a dress of pale bridegroom. She was attended by the hat, and carried a bouquet, the gift of the pink taffeta silk and a large dark blue bridegroom's two little nieces.

Kentish paper

All the bridesmaids wore red roses.

Birmingham paper

A reception was held at the home of the groom and the happy couple left afterwards for their honeymoon at Coleshill near Birmingham. The bride travelled in her birthday outfit.

Blaydon Courier

Many other brides in the collection are scheduled as ancient monuments.

Bath paper

The service was conducted by the Rev. Charles H —, M.A., the bridegroom. The wedding was of a quiet nature owing to the recent death of the bride.

Blackpool Times

One of the mourners fell dead at the graveside and this cast a gloom over the proceedings.

Gloucester paper

IT MUST BE TRUE

The Bishop of Lichfield will conduct the baptismal service at St. Chad's Church next Sunday morning at eleven o'clock.
TO READERS. You will assist The Mercury and the district generally by patronising our advertisers whenever possible.

Lichfield Mercury

We come now to the vexed question of dying, which is one that every woman has to consider if she lives long enough.

Sunday Times

R— L— (with whom P— has collaborated for the last eight years) is expecting to become a father for the first time in three months.

Hollywood Citizen News

The bride wore an ivory georgette dress with a Brussels net veil. The bridegroom wore the D.S.O.

South London paper

Miss Yolande Lessard, sister of the bride, was maid of honor and wore a white ninon skirt, matching ostrich plumes in her hair and carried a royal blue brother of the bride, and Marcel. The bridegroom was attended by his velvet muff covered with pink roses.

Portland Press Herald

The marriage of Miss Anna Bloch and Mr. Willis Dashwood, which was announced in this paper a few weeks ago, was a mistake and we wish to correct.

Colorado paper

WEDDING. AT ST. MARY'S CHURCH. CAPTAIN B— TO VIOLENT VERA, DAUGHTER OF MR. AND MRS. J. B. L—.

Calcutta paper

Hugh and Ruth went to country high-school together in Kansas, and their marriage will stop a romance begun between them there.

West Virginia paper

Mrs. Smithson – cheque and magnifying glass.

From a list of wedding presents

Mr. Thorbury was born in Victoria and immediately entered the engineering profession.

Vancouver paper

DEATHS – EDGEWORTH. On March 16th, Margaret, mother of Tom (by accident). Funeral 3.30 p.m. Tuesday.

Western Mail

To William and Kay Stout Martin, a son,
Arthur Richard Jr., on February 21.
To William and Kay Stout Martin, a son,
William Garrett, on March 16.

Wilson Alumnae Quarterly

Twin baby boys, aged 12 months, arrived at Folkestone
yesterday unconcerned, after a rough Channel crossing in
a wooden box fitted with cushions.

Sunday paper

In our last week's issue we announced the birth of a son to Mr. and Mrs. Gilbert Parkinson. We regret any annoyance that this may have caused.

Indian paper

This picture shows the 'Blizzard Baby' who was born in a hospital parking lot unnoticed by her father and mother, who collapsed as she stepped from an automobile.

American Weekly

Mr. and Mrs. A. P. Hageman are rejoicing over the arrival of a mafwpy cmfwyp emfwpy cmfpwpp doing nicely.

Florida paper

January 20th, at Kenyon Road, Wavertree, to Mr. and Mrs. Oswald Unsworth, a son (bath well).

Liverpool paper

Due to an error Mr. and Mrs. S. E. Ankrum, 104 West Healey St., are the parents of a girl, born Tuesday morning in the Mercy Hospital.

Illinois paper

Katherine Riddell was born at the
little village of Peasley. Her mother
was living there at the time.

Local paper

Mrs. George Earl, who gave birth to a 19-year-old daughter
is reported as getting along fine. A. J. Dill of Farley, who
suffered a broken leg in the same accident, is recovering.

Moran Times, Tennessee

Mrs. David Miller has a new baby boy at her house. Dave
is just as happy as if it was his.

Ohio paper

The bride carried a handsome bouquet of harem lilies.

North London paper

The bridegroom's mother wore pale gray chiffon with V-
neck, short sleeves, and skirt having a cascade down the
front. With it she wore Harvard University with the Head
of the division of chemistry, and returned to Cleveland
only a few days ago.

Cleveland paper

The bride was attended by her sister and Miss — as bridesmaids, all being very strongly under the influence of drink. VERY CHOICE – James Brothers' Coffee.

Birmingham paper

On Monday Councillor Thomson's son will be married to the eldest daughter of Councillor James. The members of the Corporation are invited to the suspicious event.

Suffolk paper

The bride was dressed in a light place in the Wesley Temple in Minneapolis, with Dr. James Brankburg, pastor, officiating.

Iowa paper

The bride will be supported by five piers.

Evening Standard

Here the couple stood, facing the floral setting and exchanged cows.

California paper

Appropriate music was played on the organ
by Mr. G. E. satin with pearl trimming.
Her train was that on earth do dwell'
and 'Father, now Thy grace extending.'
The bride was becomingly attired in
white Good. The hymns sung were 'All
people of silver lace, and she wore a
tulle veil, which had been used at her
mother's wedding.

Local paper

The bride wore a gown of white sheer with lace
insects.

Cleveland paper

The bridegroom travelled in a two-piece clerical gray
angora, striped with red and beige, worn with a black
Robin Hood hat, trimmed with red.

Essex paper

We've got fifty Yankettes married into English nobility
right now. Some are duchesses. Some are countesses.
Eleven are baronesses. Only one is a lady.

Boston Globe

Mrs. Edgar Ramsden was rushed to Roanoke Hospital on
Monday of this week for observation and treatment prior
to becoming an expectant mother.

Virgina paper

Our morality rate in Fairfield is low while our birthrate is high.

Alabama paper

```
DELTS, Colorado. When Mrs. A. S.
Glassiter, 82, died recently she was
on a basis of the acreage planted, was
survived by her husband, 13 bushels
less than the normal yield children,
80 grandchildren and 25 great-
grandchildren.
```

Staten Island Advance

His mother died when he was seven years old, while his father lived to be nearly a centurion.

Wallasey and Wirral Chronicle

BIRTH, DEATHS, AND MIRAGES

National Daily

Births. In Sherburne, October 6, a son, 10 pounds, Frederick Albert, to Mr and Mrs Russell L. and Nancy (Johnson) Stocker.

Vermont Standard

ANIMALS

Two whippet pups for sale, 9 ft ¥ 9 ft 6 in, all fittings on skids.

Shropshire Journal

There have been times when I used to follow a lonely white-eye in the forest singing lustily all the time, hopping from tree to tree, as though calling for a mate.

American Cage-Bird Magazine

IF YOU ARE WILLING TO PAY JUST A
LITTLE MORE AND ARE LOOKING FOR
A REALLY FASCINATING, OUT-OF-THE-
ORDINARY PET, MAY WE SUGGEST
YOU TRY THE SECOND FLOOR AND
ASK TO SEE OUR MISS MARTIMORE.

Sign in Toronto store, quoted in Daily Mirror

In many parts of Co. Sligo hares are now practically unknown because of the unreasonable laughter to which they have been subjected in recent years.

Sligo paper

Airedales – House-trained, safe with children, best protection against burglars or ladies living alone.

Ad in animal paper

The Ministry of Agriculture said: 'Everything is two to three weeks ahead in the farming world. Best lot of lambs we've seen in years and they will soon be pulling rhubarb.'

Daily Mail

Sir, – In reply to Mr Yarham's letter in Saturday's Eastern Daily Press, I would like to point out that the cuckoo heard by my niece on Saturday week and the one I heard and saw on Monday was not riding a cycle when I saw it fly out of a tree.

Eastern Daily Press

Cat carrying basket urgently required.

Heaton Chapel Guardian

PARROT DISEASE FEARS
R.S.P.C.A. WILL ARRANGE
PAINLESS END
FOR OWNERS OF BIRDS

Essex paper

Dear Sir,
We are always glad to advise on humane means
of destruction for any species, but in your case I
think that this would hardly be necessary.

Letter from animal welfare organization

One main event in London was Cruft's Dog Show.
For two days dogs and dog-owners from all over
the country crowded the huge halls and galleries,
barking at one another in fierce competition.

Aberdeen Press and Journal

We make a speciality of gorillas and chimpanzees. They
are wonderfully intelligent and can be trained right up to
the human standard in all except speech. One of our
directors, Mr Alec Jackson and his wife are both able to
be tamed to live in captivity.

Irish paper

The troupes of monkeys are guaranteed to keep patrons
laughing, riding bicycles, and balancing on huge balls.

Hawaiian paper

**PEDIGREE ALSATIAN PUP PIES, PRICE
10 GUINEAS EACH.**

Ad in weekly paper

The young of the hoatzin, a curious fowl-like bird native to South America, are remarkable in having clawed fingers on their wings by means of which they are able to climb about in trees like quadruplets.

Georgia paper

COLLIE DOG, 1 year old, for sale, will work sheep or cattle, hunt out any distance and stop to whistle; price £8.

The Scottish Farmer

The Tasmanian wolf is striped like a tiger, has a tail like a rat, is a relative of opossums, and is the youngest man ever to be president of the United States.

Bridgewater (Conn.) Telegraph

DOG BETS TO GET MONEY FOR MARRIAGE

Headline in Surrey paper

Bloodhounds are sometimes crossed with coon-hounds and the progeny are flying the mail between St. Louis and Chicago.

Australian paper

Riding at speed on their bicycles, dogs frequently chase the boys – and in some cases the owners think it is amusing.

African paper

Recent tests conducted by a zoologist prove that grasshoppers hear with their legs. In all cases the insects hopped when a tuning fork was sounded nearby. There was no reaction to this stimulus, however, when the insects' legs had been removed.

Corning Glass Works Magazine

A Jersey heifer aged 26 months and owned by Mr. E. Loxmore, was left in a very weak condition last week-end after giving birth to quadrupeds.

Korumburra Times

Everything is done in a sheltered house, barn or shed; in fact one can run 1,000 chickens up to fattening or killing stage in a pair of carpet slippers.

Sussex paper

FOR SALE. Thirty cross-bred hens ready to lay three shillings and sixpence apiece.

Natal Witness

The tiger came towards me bellowing and grunting, and when he got opposite the screen he gave one of those fearful coughs which only the man who has been close to such a beast can appreciate. It was eleven feet long.

Evening Standard

Any owner whose dog shows signs of illness should be chained up securely.

Bradford paper

Sir Hugh and Lady C— received many congratulations after their horse's success. The latter wore a yellow frock trimmed with picot-edged frills and a close-fitting hat.

Berkshire paper

Lady offers stylish well-cut apparel, reducing corset, waist 29, for Alsatian dog.

Women's paper

FEED YOUR DOG AS YOU WOULD FEED YOUR FRIEND. GIVE HIM BLANK'S BISCUITS.

Ad in Essex paper

They took with them an Irish terrier dog and a brown sheep dog – both pets. Both were wearing horn-rimmed glasses.

Manchester paper

She cried out in agony. And at that instant she heard a horse whisper behind her.

Indian paper

MISSING, part-Persian cat, brown and orange. Finder rewarded, dead or alive.

Ad in Yorks paper

GOOD HORSE, COMPLETE WITH
SADDLE AND BRIDLE, 6 VOLT
BATTERY, PISTONS, CONNECTING
RODS, ETC.

Ad in Nigerian Times

'We saw 26 deer come down to feed,' sighed Helen Bowman, and added that they were wearing warm sweaters at the time.

Miami Herald

Colonel Hamilton said there had been no appreciable increase in the number of lions within the last three years and he attributed this to the higher morality among young lions.

South African paper

Dyke stated in his complaint that the defendant owned a large dog that walked the floor most of the night, held noisy midnight parties, and played the radio so that sleep was impossible.

Australian paper

CAPITAL PET ANIMAL HOSPITAL — DOGS CALLED FOR, FLEAS REMOVED AND RETURNED TO YOU FOR $10.00.

Ad in Washington paper

After Mick the Miller had won the Greyhound Derby at the White City, he advanced across the track, garbed in a dinner jacket and a bowler hat, to present the prize to the owner.

West London paper

COW SAVES A LIFE
HAULS FARMER BY TAIL FROM
BLAZING BUILDING

Sussex paper

NOTICE

F. J. BATTICK, CBM, HAS BEEN APPOINTED TO EXTERMINATE ALL MONGOOSE ON THE STATION, AND HAS BEEN AUTHORISED TO DESTROY ANY OF THESE ANIMALS FOUND ABOUT THE STATION USING AN AIR RIFLE.

U.S. Naval Air-station order

FLIES COMING INTO CONTACT WITH THIS PREPARATION OF D.D.T. DIE WITHOUT HOPE OF RECOVERY.

Label on bottle

WANTED – Man to take care of cow that does not smoke or drink.

ad in South Carolina paper

Great care must always be exercised on
tethering horses to trees, as they are apt
to bark, and hereby destroy the trees.

Army order

Woofey, the rough-haired terrier belonging to Mrs.
Perkins of Boundary Road, wags his tail at the
shop doorway until Mr. Bert Williams, who keeps
the shop for his father, picks up the meat in his
mouth and takes it home.

Norfolk paper

Mr. G—, who presided, said that the time for dual purpose breeding of cattle had gone. They should breed for milk and beer separately.

Edinburgh paper

Miss Nellie Peters received painful injuries yesterday from the talons of a large horned owl which she captured in her bare hands. She will be stuffed and mounted and put on display on Main Street.

Elder (Pennsylvania) Gazette

30,000 pigeons were released filling the air with the flutter of a million wings.

Commentary in a news film

```
I was terrified . . . There was a
tiger crouching, ready to bounce.
```

Short story

This week three crows landed at Cardiff who had been sunk by submarines twice, and in some cases three times.

Manchester Guardian

Before its late summer departure the sparrow will build several nests and will bear many little sparrows, judging from past performances.

Mrs. Hetherington said that she had not had the same luck with male birds.

The Sun

STOCKINGS DOWN AGAIN
WANTED: FAT CALVES

Ad in Jersey paper

The first few days the chicks were fed inside the brooder house on pieces of asbestos concrete sheets, 3ft. long by 2 ft. wide.

Poultry article

LOST. Friday night between Market Square and Dimsdale Avenue, Black and White terrier. Name and address on collar of owner.

ad in local paper

It is scandalous to see these Society women going about with a poodle dog on the end of a string where a baby would be more fitting.

New Zealand paper

WANTED, A GENT'S OR LADY'S
BICYCLE FOR A PURE BRED SABLE
AND WHITE COLLIE.

Lincolnshire paper

LOCAL NEWS

Baby Show. – Best Baby under Six Months; Best Baby under Twelve Months; Best Baby under Two Years; Best Baby under Three Years. Rules for Exhibitors:– All Exhibits become the property of the Committee as soon as staged, and will be sold for the benefit of the Hospital at the termination of the exhibition.

Exhibition programme

. . . and a few moments after the Countess had broken the traditional bottle of champagne on the bows of the noble ship, she slid slowly and gracefully down the slipway, entering the water with scarcely a splash.

Essex paper

He had the privilege also of viewing a number of rare Egyptian tummies.

Cleveland (Ohio) paper

The Fitzhenrys had come to South Africa in the forties. At that time he was forty and she was twenty-nine. He was now fifty and she was twenty-nine.

South African Weekly

George B— had charge of the entertainment during the past year. His birth-provoking antics were always the life of the party and he will be greatly missed.

Willard (Ohio) Times, Ohio

Princess Margaret, wearing a summery yellow-ribbed cotton dress, white brimmed hat covered with daisies and yellow sandals, was shown round the laboratories.

Oxford Times

Zanuck, in his speech, showed great humility and told briefly of his beginning here in our midst. But he didn't reflect on his early struggles; how, when he wrote and wrote and got one rejection after the other and could not even get into a studio, he had to take a job down at Wilmington catching hot rivets in the shipbuilding plant to eat.

Hollywood Reporter

Just to keep the record straight, it was the famous Whistler's Mother, not Hitler's, that was exhibited at the recent meeting of Pleasantville Methodists. There is nothing to be gained in trying to explain how the error occurred.

Titusville (Pa.) Herald

The winner of the competition to guess the number of sweets in the jar was Mrs— who will therefore travel to Majorca by air, spend five days in a luxury hotel (all inclusive) and fly home via Paris, without any need to spend a penny.

Announcement in a Westmorland church magazine

The after-lunch talk was given by Mr Derek Wigram – school headmaster retired, but now serving the Lord in an advisory capacity.

Crusade

Winners in the home-made claret section were Mrs Davis (fruity, well-rounded), Mrs Rayner (fine colour and full-bodied), and Miss Ogle-Smith (slightly acid, but should improve if laid down).

From a Leicestershire parish magazine

A jumble sale will be held in the Parish Room on Saturday 27th September. This is a chance to get rid of anything that is not worth keeping but is too good to throw away. Don't forget to bring your husbands.

St. Ambrose (Lancs.) Parish Magazine

The other day Sarah went to Victory House to make a speech for War Bonds and not only inspired one service man to buy $1,000 worth, another one $500, but she sold herself and purchased a $50 bond.

Los Angeles Times

The service ended with the singing of the good old hymn: 'All police that on earth do dwell.'

Canadian paper

The Ladies' Benevolent Association held its regular monthly meeting on Monday evening. Mr. Watts made a motion that he would take care of any ladies present who wished to discard any clothing.

North Spur (California) Sentinel

Mr. Barden spoke with an eloquence which sprang from his deep-seated conviction of the grave pass which we have reached, basing his proposals upon the significant memorandum which the Almighty had prepared at his request.

Montreal Gazette

Slough Borough babies have their big change at the baby show. Entries can be made on the ground and during the evening the last eight will contest the Berks and Bucks darts championship.

Windsor, Slough & Eton Express

Usually the annual effort is a sale of work and a concert, but this year so as not to put too great a strain upon supporters, a concert and a sale of work have been arranged.

Exeter Express and Echo

The native inhabitants produce all manner of curios, the great majority of which appear to command a ready sale among the visitors, crude and commonplace as they frequently are.

Bulawayo Chronicle

Among those present, with whom his Lordship shook hands very cordially were three men, one armless.

Daily Mail

As formerly, the ticket-holders, with their numbers, were placed in a barrel and thoroughly shaken up.

Hamilton Advertiser

The procession will be composed for the Ledbury Urban Council Boy Scouts, Girl Guides, Girls consist of English meat and an allowance of two glasses of beer per head, or minerals as desired.

Local paper

An interesting address on 'The National Care of the Child' by Miss Palmer was much appreciated by all, and Mrs. Lever in a short address made an appeal for the use of the humane killer.

Berkshire paper

Mrs. Raymond Hackett and Miss Evelyn Fothergill gave a surprise pink and white shower for Mrs. Mahlon Owens on the Eaton Lawn, attended by 33 people. One feature of the program was a Caesarian operation which proved amusing.

Vermont paper

POTTERY STALL – MRS. D— AND MISS N—. BOTH USEFUL AND ORNAMENTAL.

Garden fête programme

During the interval the huge park was full of the local gentry that arrived in hundreds of cars and ate excellent home-made cakes under an enormous marquise.

Manchester paper

The Women's Club annual costume party was held last week. The ladies were asked to come dressed like tramps and that was easy for most of them.

Louisville Courier-Journal

YOUNG PEOPLE'S SOCIETY. Everyone is invited. Tea and Social Hour at 6.15. Mrs. Smith will sin.

St. Louis church programme

A well-rounded ladies programme is now in process of being worked up.

> Journal of the Electro-chemical Society

Out of over 40 entries the following emerged as winners: Pet with the most amusing appearance . . . Mrs. C. Smith.

> Birmingham paper

All members will participate in the annual club luncheon. Owing to the large numbers it is deemed desirable to eat on the first day those whose surnames commence with any letters from A to M.

> South African paper

A cake-making demonstration by Mrs. Jacobs was followed by a talk on poisons and their antidotes by a local chemist.

> Australian paper

Last night the Stephen C. Fishers quite outdid themselves at the Ritz-Carlton when they presented their Elizabeth at a ball disguised – and successfully too – as an Italian terrace and garden.

> New York paper

The Countess of — who was with a merry party wore nothing to indicate that she was a holder of four Scottish titles.

Scottish paper

Mr. and Mrs. Wally Burman of Sioux Falls have just arrived at the Lindau home where they will be housepests for several days.

Minnesota paper

The public will be allowed to inspect the Crematorium on Sundays. Other amusements will be found advertised in the local Press.

Canadian paper

SIR WILLIAM RAMSAY'S POSER STARTLES AUDIENCE

London, February 4th. Sir William Ramsay raised the question whether the unfit should be left to die at the annual dinner of the Institute of Sanitary Engineers tonight.

Montreal Gazette

Mrs. Joe Sexton and children, of deadwood Gulch, were guests of the A. Dennys family on Sunday.
Mrs. Dennys is almost confined to her bed with nervous exhaustion.

Idaho paper

Mr. Asquith was accompanied by Mrs. Asquith and the audience singing 'For he's a jolly good Lady Bonham-Carter'.

Scottish paper

Mrs Thurston Longson and daughters are planning to tour the Black Hills, Yellowstone Park and other places of interest. They are taking a tent and cooking utensils and will vamp by the side of the road.

South Dakota paper

Mr and Mrs Fred Upton returned Thursday from a visit in the tropics. The rest and change of climate has done them both good. Mrs Upton looks healthier and lonelier than ever.

New England weekly

Mr William Duncan of North Dakota stopped here on his way to Fostoria to say hell to his many friends today.

Medina (Ohio) Sentinel

KENNETH HARLAN, FILM ACTOR, SAID TO HAVE BEEN SEEN WITH WIFE

Headline in Portland Oregonian

THE CHURCH

Soloist at the Trinity Y.P.U. meeting referred to on Saturday, Miss McCausland sang the solo, Lord Speak To Me, not Miss McDonald.

Canadian paper

THIS IS THE GATE OF HEAVEN
ENTER YE ALL BY THIS DOOR
THIS DOOR IS KEPT LOCKED
BECAUSE OF THE DRAUGHT

Seen at Cumberland church

Spring Flower and Egg Service Address by Rev. Edwin Strange Parents and adult fiends are especially invited.

Waveney Chronicle

Will parishes who so far have made no payment do so without fail before the end of the year and so save my grey hairs. There are 68 of them at the time of writing.

Diocesan Magazine

He believed that with the assistance of the ladies it would be possible to form a non-profit-making concern.

Church magazine

THE CHURCH

The Rev. R. H. Maidstone made his first appearance in the pulpit at Palmerston Street Church, Castletown, on Sunday evening. The choir gave the anthem: 'Who is This, So Weak.'

Isle of Man Examiner

It is unfortunately true of this age, as with every other age, that the poor can be defrauded with impunity, the Archbishop said.
See Banham Bros. List of used car bargains on page 9.

Hants paper

We sent sixty dresses to Miss Forsythe in December, and we have just heard that she is using our gift in roofing the Mission House.

Annual Report of the Hibernian Church Missionary Society

Rev J. Towney Davis has spoken in the largest Baptist churches in America. To miss hearing him will be the chance of a lifetime.

Raleigh (N Carolina) News & Observer

God is Always At hand To Help in Adversity. Please write Box 3092.

> Border Counties Advertiser

Very Rev M. Canon D—, ugly and unsightly debris heap, was being transformed into a delightful miniature park.

> Limerick Chronicle

For some time past running water has been installed at the cemetery to the satisfaction of the inhabitants.

> Républicain Lorrain

Our own Bishop has promised to take the chair. There will be a very strong platform to support him.

> Diocesan Magazine

HYMN 326 'Stand Up, Stand Up for Jesus!'
(Congregation seated)

> Michigan Church leaflet

At 6.45 p.m., at the Young People's meeting, there will be a review of the first eight chapters of the Book of the Acts. The review will be in the form of a baseball game.

> Battle Creek (Michigan) Enquirer

The Women's Society of Christian Service of the Methodist Church entertained the senior girls and teachers of Yale schools with a tea Tuesday afternoons. Guests were revived from 4 p.m. to 5 p.m. in the home of Mrs. John Dennis.

Cushion (Oklahoma) Daily Citizen

It would be a great help towards keeping the churchyard in good order if others would follow the example of those who clip the grass on their own graves.

Parish magazine

Dear Member,
Just a reminder that the fourth Friday
noon of February is next Monday,
February 28th.

Church circular

THERE WILL BE A PROCESSION NEXT
SUNDAY AFTERNOON IN THE
GROUNDS OF THE MONASTERY; BUT
IF IT RAINS IN THE AFTERNOON, THE
PROCESSION WILL TAKE PLACE IN
THE MORNING

Notice in Irish church

One of the exquisite features was the presence of
the Deacon's wives. We had 83 upon our Roll of
Honour, and of these 36 turned up.

Parish magazine

**A PARSON LOOKS BACK
THE EFFECT OF A CLERICAL COLLAR.**

Esher News and Advertiser

The hymns 'Love Divine' and 'O Perfect Love' were sung
whilst the organist played a Wedding March.

Surrey paper

It was announced today that the wedding would take place on July 3rd at St. Mary's Church. Betting 9-4 against, 6-1, 10-1.

Durham paper

EXPENDITURE ON CHOIR OUTINGS
Deficit from last year, owing to the vicar, £1. 5.6.

Parish Magazine

BRUNSWICK CHAPEL
10.30 REV. FRANK JACKSON
6.30 REV. MARK RADLEY
'THE MOST HOPELESS YOUNG MEN IN LEEDS.'

Yorkshire Post

Here the party was courteously received by Miss B—, secretary to the Rev. Canon R— (who, owing to absence, was unable to be present).

Manchester City News

I write on behalf of the Churchwardens to state we think it desirable to make a change in the arrangements for keeping the grass in order, as Mr. Bazely is now getting very infirm. We have given him notice to expire at Christmas.

West Sussex County Times

THE CHURCH

That other famous Christian hymn 'Hark, the herald angels sing' was originally written 'Hark, how all the author, John Byrom, who lived in 1745, had a favourite daughter, Dolly.

Glasgow Evening Citizen

'How dreadful is this place.' This melodious, thoroughly diatonic little piece is specially adapted for the dedication of a church.

Musical Times

A familiar question was re-opened –
How Sunday School children are to be
attached to the Church, and once more
the use of adhesive stamps was
recommended.

New Zealand Church News

An 'At Home' was held at the Vicarage last evening, the first of a series arranged in aid of the fund for providing red cossacks for the choir.

Birmingham paper

Bishop Sherrill conducted the first part of the simple Episcopal ceremony, and Dr. Peabody took it up at the point where the couple exchanged their cows.

New York paper

Come of the GOSPEL HALL
67 Victoria Street, tomorrow night at 8.30
and hear of
'HELL – Where it is; what it's like.'
Lighting, seating, heating, and shelter provided
for all who wish to come inside. No collection.

Announcement in Belfast Telegraph

The Rev. J. R.— has derived great benefit from his holiday abroad and is returning this week to his cuties.

New Zealand paper

ADDRESS (10 MINUTES) . . . REV. J.
B. C.——
ANTHEM . . . 'IT IS ENOUGH' —
HANDEL.

Church notice board

THE CHURCH

We are most grateful to those who so
kindly repaired the dilapidated hassocks
for the Church. Let us kneel on them.
                              Wiltshire Church paper

PROGRAMME
3.0 Hymns of Praise. Films.
3.45 'HUNGARY MEN'
4.15 Question Time
4.30 Tea and buns (1s. per person).
6.0 'I was HUNGRY - SICK'.
6.45 'WHAT DO WE DO?' Open Forum.
7.45 Prayers.
                    London Missionary Society Programme

The trial board of the North-West Synod of the United
Lutheran Church last night found the Rev. Victor
Hutchings, 39, guilty on five of six counts of heresy. It
recommended that he should be suspended from his pulpit
at Gethsemane Church, Brookfield, Wisconsin.

                                        Daily Telegraph

The Bishop of -- has announced his
engagement by cable.
May I ask for your loyalty and co-operation in
the difficult times ahead?

                          Vicar's Letter in parish magazine

The service was conducted by the Rev.—. After the Benedictine, Mr. and Mrs. — sang 'I'll walk beside you.'

Report of wedding

THE INTERESTING ANNOUNCEMENT IS MADE THAT FINCHDALE PRIORY HAS BEEN HANDED OVER TO THE SOCIETY FOR THE PREVENTION OF ANCIENT MONUMENTS.

Provincial paper

```
HYMN . . . No. 336
(Congregation standing)
SERMON, 'What are you standing for?' -
Dr. Fosdick.
```

New York Church Bulletin

Owing to the continued illness of the Vicar, which we trust is reaching its last stage, the services have been conducted by the Rev.—

New Zealand Diocesan Magazine

The new automatic couplings fitted to the organ will enable Mr.— to change his combinations without moving his feet.

Parish Magazine

The age limit for Girl Guides was formerly 18 years, but by general request it has now been raised to 81 years.

Morning paper

Its lone peal summons the faithful to worship while the others are dismantled and repaired.

Bucks Advertiser

Once this work is completed, the stained windows will be put back into their frames and the pews will be replaced. Good progress is being made by the workmen of Messrs. Jackson, Builders, McGregor, Marshall, Brown, Murray (Captain), and Thompson. Reserves: Green and Morrison. Kick-off 2.15.

Northumberland paper

IN THE KITCHEN

To serve, dip moulds in water to loosen the contents and serve with passion fruit and cream. British housewives can substitute pineapple, cherries or apricots for passion.

Romford Recorder

Too often is a birthday made nothing more than an occasion for present giving and a party. It should have another side to it, if it is truly to be the subject for congratulations, small balls, flour and fry in boiling fat.

Hants paper

The principal thing to remember when preparing a fork supper is to select only food which can be eaten comfortably on a plate with a fork. In the winter, hot bouillon or clear soup is always popular and can well be included.

Sunday paper

The way to his heart might lie in the tricky art of cooking his liver.

She, cookery supplement

Whether you eat 'em as breakfast folls or with supper you'll keep on eating till the box is empty! Oh my, but they do taste good.

Pittsburgh Post-Gazette

They are selling whole chickens and portions already cooked, in wine, at 6s 3d a pound. All that is needed is to eat the chicken, while still sealed in the bag.

Liverpool Echo

OWING TO A PRINTER'S ERROR IN THE 'FAIRY-RING' CAKE RECIPE LAST WEEK 'TWO OUNCES CASTOR OIL' WAS GIVEN FOR 'TWO OUNCES CASTER SUGAR'. WE APOLOGIZE FOR THIS SILLY MISTAKE.

Reveille

We forwarded your enquiry re nettle tea to the writer of the recipe in our issue of July 20th, but have received a notification from his executors' solicitors to say that he is now deceased.

Gardening paper

Coo forty-five minutes and cover with a layer of sliced tomatoes. Season lightly with salt and pepper and coo until meat is very tender.

Beverly Hills Shopping News

Add the remainder of the milk, beat again, turn quickly into buttered pans and bake half an hour. Have the oven hot, twist a length of narrow green ribbon around them and you have a pretty bouquet for your dress or hat.

Barrow News

Save time and cut fingers with a parsley mincer.

> This Week

EGGS FOR SALE. WHY GO OUT OF
BEDFORD TO BE SWINDLED? COME
TO THE – POULTRY FARM.

> Ad in Bedford paper

The best plan is to hold the bottle firmly and
remove the cook as gently as possible.

> Women's paper

Pickled Pork or Boiled Rabbi. . . . 2s. 3d.

Café menu

Drop hat cooked rice into hot soap by spoonfuls and you will have rice dumplings.

Indiana paper

20 Dozens Bottles excellent Old Tawny Port, sold to pay for charges, the owner having been lost sight of, and bottled by us last year.

Wine merchant's catalogue

Built on the lines of an old farmhouse kitchen, French girls in picturesque costumes flit about with cups of coffee and liqueurs.

The Motor Cycle

CHEAP SPONGE ROLL
TAKE A TEACUPFUL OF FLOUR AND MIX IT
WITH A TEACUPFUL OF CASTER SUGAR
AND A TEASPOONFUL OF BAKING
POWDER; BREAK TWO EGGS INTO A CUP,
THEN SLIDE INTO THE MIXTURE.

Bristol Times and Mirror

Some people do not know that they can be treated exactly like chipped potatoes, that is, cut in thin slices and fried in deep fat.

Liverpool paper

This butter, manufactured from the best cream, will stand any high temperature if kept in a cool place.

Bombay catalogue

HEALTH BISCUITS
Nice and Tasty
Handled by our
55 salesmen daily

Ad in Montreal Star

After removing the meat from your broiling pan allow it to soak in soapy water.

Seattle Post-Intelligence

DUE TO A COPY ERROR, WE REGRET THAT THE SURPRISE APPLE SWEET POTATO RECIPE IN THE OCTOBER ISSUE WAS INCOMPLETE. PLEASE ADD: 4 CUPS OF MASHED SWEET POTATOES AND 3 LARGE APPLES.

Cannery publication

RESTAURANT SUR LA MER
AUJOURD'HUI . . . L'IRIS-STEW À
L'ECOSSAISE.

Notice outside French restaurant

SIR, your correspondent suggests that the bones of the herring be first removed, then offered for retail sale. I have found that in actual practice this does not appeal to the housewife.

Brighton paper

TODAY'S FRENCH MENU – Marconi au gratin.

Kent paper

When this is done, sit on a very hot stove and stir frequently.

Cookery book

HALF FRESH LOBSTER . . .

Pleasure steamer menu

For coping with unexpected guests, it is always a good plan to keep a few tons of sardines in the house.

Women's paper

QUICKLY MADE SOUP – Required: 4lbs. fat, 3/4 lb. caustic soda, 10 ozs. Resin, 9 pints of water.

Sunday paper

SPECIAL TODAY – STEWED TEAK AND POTATOES.

Menu in East End café

A chicken thief was reported active on Wednesday night, and at the Bennett J. Dickerman property a score of fine chickens were taken from the poultry house. The matter was reported at police headquarters and is being investigated.

A chicken pie supper will be served by the Ladies' Aid Society in Centreville parish house on Thursday at 6 o'clock.

New Haven Journal-Courier

Never crumble your bread or roll in the soup.

Etiquette book

Break the eggs carefully into a basin taking care
not to break the eggs.

Cookery book

LADY WILL EXCHANGE CLOTHING,
SELF, LITTLE GIRL, FOR FARM
BUTTER, EGGS, JAM.

Ad in The Lady

It's a fine scene, denoting 'Eat, Drink, and be merry, tomorrow we 'Eat, drink, and be merry for tomorrow we
lose its spontaneous significance.

Liverpool paper

THERE IS NO SUBSTITUTE FOR OUR COFFEE
SO DO NOT TRY IT
OTHERS HAVE TO THEIR SORROW

Ad in Canadian paper

*My lunch these days consists of a chair in the
park and the Daily Mail.*

Letter in the Daily Mail

At next Wednesday's children's party it is expected that in two hours 300 children will consume 1,800 sandwiches and 900 fancy cakes, gallons of milk and tea, pounds of butter and a fishfryer, a plumber, a schoolmaster, and a railway inspector.

Yorkshire Gazette

Wash beets very clean, then boil. When done, swim out into a pan of cold water and slip the skins off with the fingers.

Boston Globe

Gen. Graham, who likes to eat as well as any man, would like to see a bit more cor bread ad mustard brees served to the President at the 'wite White House' at this aval submari statio.
'Don't get me wrong,' he cautioned.

World Telegram and Sun

WILD FOODS OF GREAT BRITAIN WITH 46 FIGS.

Times Literary Supplement

MEDICAL &
SCIENTIFIC

A study by three physicians showed that perhaps two out of three births in the U.S. result from pregnancies.

Columbus (Ohio) Citizen

News From The Hospitals
Admitted: Gay Tufarolo, 107 Main Street.
Discouraged: Mrs Elizabeth Cook, Holly Hill.

Daytona Beach Evening News

Among the side reactions of this mercurial drug the most important is the death of the patient shortly after the injection.

New York State Medical Journal

If the patient faints when standing up he collapses on to the ground.

First-Aid manual

Practise the art of deep breathing. After the morning bath take a deep breath, retain it as long as possible, then slowly expire.

Home Chat

IN VIEW OF THE TYPHOID EPIDEMIC, HOTEL
GUESTS ARE ASSURED THAT ALL
VEGETABLES HAVE BEEN BOILED IN WATER
SPECIALLY PASSED BY THE MANAGER.

Notice in Cyprus hotel

The *Sagona*'s doctors and nurses were scheduled to land
last night, but messages indicated that the men probably
would be married aboard the ship, receive first-aid
treatment, and then be taken to St John's.

New York World-Telgram

Experts know that the alcoholic process takes longer in
the men, but the end result is the same.

Daily Record

Mrs George was married before anaesthetics came into
use in surgical operations.

Ludlow (Indiana) Tribune

The doctor smiled reassuringly at the worried
mother and patted her little bot on the cheek.

Paperback book

A man who had lost his right leg in 1946 bought eighteen pairs of shoes in the next twenty years – and never used the left ones.

Reveille

Captain Thompson said that the epidemic of laryngitis among men might be traced to the development of central heating in London hotels and restaurants and the scantiness of women's attire.

Kent paper

General practitioners were responsible for more than 80 per cent of the hospital confinements of borough mothers.

Report of a Medical Officer of Health

```
The dispensary, however, will be open
in the afternoon from one-thirty to
four on Monday to Friday for
decapitated students with the nurse in
charge.
```

Pomona College Student Life

Mrs. Oscar Maddox is able to be up after being confined to bed for several weeks with malaria fever, to the delight of her friends.

Thomasville (Georgia) Times-Enterprise

London, July – Mrs. Annie Besant, eighty-year-old theosophist, was confined to bed today at the home of friends at Wimbledon. A severe child forced her to cancel all lecture engagements.

Houseton Chronicle

Miss Georgina P. Mathie, principal psychologist, County of Stirling, quoted the case of a nine-year-old boy who ran amok with a hatchet in the large family of which he was a member, saying, 'There are far too many bairns here.' She showed how by psychological treatment he became completely adjusted and several years later was working a guillotine in a printer's establishment.

Ross-shire Journal

After being free from Rheumatic Fever for 30 years I commenced taking your pills.

Provincial paper

Dr. S— has been appointed Resident Medical Officer to the Mater Misericordiae Hospital.

Orders have been given for the immediate extension of the Glasnevin cemetery. The work is being executed with the utmost despatch.

Dublin evening paper

The doctor looked closely at the woman's face. 'It's a most peculiar thing,' he murmured.

Short story

The number of unvaccinated children born in Lambeth during the last three years averages 800 a year.

Daily paper

One man was admitted to hospital suffering from buns.

Bristol paper

Alcoholism
Dr. C. Nelson Davis will discuss this
health problem at an education meeting
of the Junior League.
On Tuesday March 18th at 7.45 p.m.
Cocktails from 6 p.m.

Lecture invitation

Have plenty of orangs in the house. They can be relied on to keep the doctor away.

Woman's paper

The operation is relatively safe, the scientists said. It has been tried on about 30 dogs. Five of them are alive and well.

The Post

Miss Dorothy Morrison, who was injured by a fall from a horse last week, is in St. Joseph's Hospital and covered sufficient to see her friends.

Morristown (N.D.) News

PUBLIC HEALTH PROBLEM
SPECIAL COMMITTEE TO SIT ON BED BUG.

Liverpool paper

Mrs. Skeffington regrets not being able to keep her appointment with Dr. James owing to sickness today at 12 o'clock as arranged.

Note received by Liverpool doctor

The Red Cross paid for emergency care and later found a free bed for her in an institution specializing in the treatment of artcritics.

Arizona Star

The healthful flow of blood through the body requires that the body be as one. If the arm were cut off from the chest, the head free of the trunk, and the leg an independent unity, the whole body would be weakened and its use impaired.

Atlanta Journal

PATIENTS WHO ARE N.C.O.s WILL WEAR THEIR CHEVRONS IF MARKED 'UP', AND IF CONFINED TO BED WILL BE PINNED TO THE WALL OF THE MARQUEE ABOVE THEIR BEDS.

Army hospital notice

It is generally agreed that human beings acquire sleeping sickness from biting flies.

The Pioneer

The *Gunaandal* came in on Saturday afternoon with 25 baskets of fish, averaging about 65lb. each, and only about 5 per cent were not edible. These were distributed among the hospitals.

Sydney Evening News

The accident caused great excitement in the neighbourhood. A large crowd quickly gathered and several medical men were hurried to the sport.

Manchester Guardian

I recommend my patients to eat the tables with their meat, and to be careful not to swallow their food too quickly.

Medical Weekly

The Nilotic race is remarkable for the disproportionately long legs of their men and women. They extend on the eastern side of the Nile right down into the Uganda Protectorate.

From a book by Sir Harry H. Johnston

BLANK'S NERVE TONIC DRIVES
AWAY NERVY SYMPTOMS, GIVES
POWER OF BRAIN AND BODY.
LEAVES BEHIND IRRITABILITY,
INDIGESTION, RHEUMATISM,
NEURALGIA, HYSTERIA, ETC.

Ad in a Time Table

REMEMBER A SNOOKS & CO.
LADDER WILL LAST TWENTY YEARS OR MORE IF
YOU DON'T WEAR OUT THE RUNGS WITH USE.

From a leaflet

After using your ointment my face started to clear up at once, and after using two jars it was gone altogether.

Ad in Bristol paper

MOTOR-BIKE, complete, less engine, frame, tank, coil, saddle, handlebar, tyres, etc.

Ad in Motor Cycling

Lie flat on the back, with the feet tucked under the wardrobe. Keep the hands at the sides and raise the legs until they are vertical. Very slowly lower again.

South African paper

Between lunch and dinner take another tumbler of cold water. Take a glass of cold water half an hour after lunch, half an hour after tea, and before going to bed at night. Never drink between meals.

Woman's Life

Dr. S— had been attending her, roughly, once a week.

Daily Mail

Dr. Gordon Nikiforuk of Toronto University told the Ontario Dental Association that a person can help prevent decay by vigorously rinsing his mother after each meal.

News telegram from Toronto

Dr. John M. Charlesworth replaced the medical equipment he took with him into the Army four and a half years ago, gave birth to a daughter at the office today and sat back to resume civilian practice.

Boston paper

Just to let you know that your patient has been booked for her confinement under Miss Watson's car, on the recommendation of the Public Health Authority.

Letter received by doctor

WE REGRET THAT OUR MEDICAL CONTRIBUTOR IS ILL AND THEREFORE NOT ABLE TO WRITE HIS WEEKLY COLUMN 'HOW TO BE HEALTHY' AT PRESENT.

North Country paper

The First Aid treatment for a broken rib is to apply a tight bandage after you have made the patient expire.

Manchester paper

The Crewe committee has arranged to apply the vaccine to 20 calves in October and three months later five or six more will be inoculated. Later some of both lots will be killed for the post-mortem examination, and if it is likely to prove beneficial, human beings will be similarly treated.

Australian paper

The address to which the patient left should be left blank if the patient has died.

M.O.H. hospital index card

The many friends of Mrs. Barrett will be sorry to learn that she injured her foot on Sunday. It will probably be six weeks before the fool can be released from a plaster cast.

Canadian paper

She is a great believer in the importance of a child having real knowledge of the body instead of allowing it to be wrapped in mystery. She has accordingly included in the book appendix giving clear details of its workings.

Book review in the Sunday Times

Although His Highness is in touch with specialist medical advisers in this country, his health remains good and his spirits excellent.

Indian paper

In answer to 'Desperate' I should advise her to take her small son to a doctor or specialist. These pests can change a well and happy child into a very miserable one.

Women's paper

No authenticated case has been known in which sterile parents have transmitted that quality to their offspring.

Letter to The Times

He was a Fellow of the Institute of Chemists, and a Fellow of the Chemises Society.

Irish paper

They were all delighted to have Miss Benson back amongst them, their best wishes would go with her next week when she set out for her holiday, and they all hoped she would return with
MEASLES AND WHOOPING-COUGH

Scottish paper

It wasn't the proper doctor – just a young locust taking his place while he was away.

Short story in the Evening News

HEADACHES? LET US EXAMINE YOUR EYES
AND HELP YOU IN REMOVING SAME.

Notice in optician's window

TEETH EXTRACTED WITH THE GREATEST PAINS

Dentist's advertisement

'The nurses who have a seven minutes' walk to their home quarters, have never had a rude word addressed to them,' said the matron, 'not even,' she added, 'when they have had too much to drink.'

Daily Province, Vancouver

Dr. W. T.— read an interesting paper on 'Idiots from Birth'. There were over two hundred present.

Surrey paper

In the preliminary examination of patients the author introduces a test that is new to us; two or three breaths having been drawn through the nose, this organ is then punched by the anaesthetist, whilst the patient holds his breath as long as possible.

The Practitioner

The increase in number and percentage of autopsies is a tribute to the energy and zeal of the hospital staff in general and to the geniality and personal charm of our chief resident Dr. George Grainer.

Annual Report of a Connecticut Hospital

On making enquiries at the Hospital this afternoon, we learn that the deceased is as well as can be expected.

Jersey Evening Post

Mrs.— wishes to thank the nurse and doctor for their kind co-operation in the loss of her husband.

North Bucks Times

The seaman, severely injured when the ship was three hours out, was taken to hospital and the hippopotamus removed.

Daily Telegraph

All the chemical elements are dissolved in sea-water. The explanation is that rivers have been carrying dissolved miners into the sea for millions of years.

Oregon paper

COUNTLESS OTHER WORLDS
Dr. Jones's argument for believing that there are countless other worlds where living beings are present, briefly, is this:
Ninety per cent of the shrimps served on the tables of the United States come from the coastal waters of Alabama, Florida, Georgia, Louisiana, Mississippi, and Texas.

Minneapolis Tribune

YOU CAN SKATE MORE THAN ONE MILE ON ONE SLICE OF BREAD

Saturday Evening Post

Electrocution of microbes is the latest dental method. The apparatus consists mainly of a violet ray, a glass tube, and an insulted sofa.

Canadian paper

Zoologists could only visit the hot springs in El Hamma with the permission of the local Kaliphat and with an escort of police, since it is reserved for the exclusive use of Muslim women bathers. An attempt was made to bring back a number of specimens alive in vacuum flasks so that further investigation could be carried out in Oxford.

Illustrated London News

A sample of milk from a churn was found to contain added water to the extent of 6½ per cent. Milk taken direct from the cow was genuine.

Essex paper

RA RA RA RA . . . Mrs. J. P. Reynolds is confined to her home on Tilney Avenue with illness.

Georgia paper

The Right Hon. John B— is now happily recovered from his recent attack of gastric hilarity, caught in a railway train.

Western People

MR. AND MISS DYMOCK HAVE GONE FOR A MONTH TO ROTORUA FOR THE BENEFIT OF MRS. DYMOCK'S HEALTH.

New Zealand Mail

It was while walking home, one raw morning, from an all-night party that she caught a child.

Irish Independent

THE SMALL ADS

100 NEW PRICE RISES
BUT GROCERS SAY THEY WILL NOT
HIT THE HOUSEWIVES

The Sun

Complete home for sale; two double, one single bed, dining-room, threepiece suite, wireless, television, carpets, lion, etc.

Ad in Portsmouth Evening News

Lost, one four-poster brass pyramid with Terylene mudguards and retractable plastic legs; reward.

Bristol Evening Post

ONE WEEK SALE OF BLANKETS
THESE BARGAIN LOTS ARE RAPIDLY SHRINKING

Ad in provincial paper.

Gents 3-speed bicycle, also two ladies for sale, in good running order.

Lancashire paper

THIS IS A GENUINE OFFER — NO CONNECTION WITH ANY OTHER FIRM WHO ARE SELLING RUBBISH.

From a circular

B–Hotel. Ideal home for married couples, temporary or permanent.

Ad in Liverpool paper

For sale. Quonset house in Douglas. Terms cash. All reasonable offers rejected.

Michigan paper

Gas range $15; washing machine $25; bird cage $4; baby cart $4; baby $15. Apply 519 E. 36th Ave.

Portland (Oregon) Shopping News

MUST SELL. PLYMOUTH 4-DOOR SEDAN,
COMPLETE WITH ACTRESS.
CALL DE 4-3855.

Ad in Philadelphia Enquirer

DO YOU WANT A PAIR OF GLOVES MADE FROM YOUR OWN SKIN?

Ad in London Weekly

For sale – Granite-faced Gentleman's residence in St Saviour's.

Ad in Jersey paper

The outbuildings include a heated greenhouse and petting shed.

Estate agent's list

WE EXCHANGE EVERYTHING —
BICYCLES, WASHING MACHINES, ETC., ETC.
BRING YOUR WIFE AND GET THE DEAL
OF YOUR LIFE.

Sign in shop window

Gentleman has several small houses let to tenants he wishes to dispose of.

Dalton's Weekly

FOAM CUSHIONS – AS AN INTRODUCTION INTO THE RUBBER TRADE WE OFFER FOAM RUBBER CUSHIONS AT ROCK BOTTOM PRICES.

Ad in Ayrshire Post

Lady in Black Velvet Dinner Gown (38 bust, 5 ft 8 in. figure), £5.

Ad in The Lady

This lovely dress in satin and lace has a matching waist-length jacket. The lace skirt comes off for less formal occasions.

Herts paper

Business lady requires Comfortable Bed Sitting room
with boar.

Ad in Lancs. paper

```
No. 69 One Pair Unique 18th cent.
Candlesticks
No. 70 Another Pair, ditto.
```

Auctioneer's catalogue

PIERCED EARS 3S 6D A PAIR

Sign in jeweller's shop

Accommodation available. Will suit two working girls,
willing to share room or young respectable working man.

Wisbech Standard

Household and miscellaneous for sale . . . High Chair
(converts to Electric Toaster) £3.10.0.

Royal Gazette, Bermuda

Furnished front airy room near bust stop suitable for
bachelors. Apply 4 Benji Road, Kuala Lumpur.

Straits Times

Ferrari . . . extensive mechanical overhaul, discs,
humorous expensive extras.

Exchange & Mart

At Southborne, well-built detached house in sheltered position yet with sea views, adjoining bus route and short walk to shops. Immediate possession. 3 good bedrooms, two spacious deception rooms.

Bournemouth Evening Echo

West Bromwich . . . Freehold House . . . fitted kitchen (sink unit, plumber in Bendix washing machine) . . .

West Bromwich Midland Chronicle and Free Press

Dover Road. Semi-det. house with sea through lounge.

Folkestone, Hythe and District Herald

Stenographer – five years legal experience, seeks permanent connexions. Late 1967 model, good shape, many extras, used for pleasure spins by private owners. A real bargain. 522 E. Broad St.

Cleveland (Ohio) News

One collapsible baby, good condition, $7.

Ad in Canadian paper

To LET — YOUNG GIRL TWO STOREYS, BEAUTIFUL BALCONY, CENTRAL HEATING, MODERATE RENT.

L'Alsace

Two-room basement apartment, hot and cold water, shower in basement. Private entrance. Almost private bath.
Ad in Lawrence (Kansas) Journal-World

LOST
Antique cameo ring, depicting Adam and Eve in Market Square Saturday night.
Ad in Essex paper

Pukerua Bay: House, fibrous plaster, 3 large bedrooms, septic tank not quite complete. Owner living in same.
Dominion (New Zealand)

Fine Opossum Pelts, dyed to look exactly like fine opossum.
Ad in Philadelphia Bulletin

DON'T DECIDE NOW. HAVE THE SET IN YOUR OWN HOME. AFTER TWO DAYS' TRIAL WE SHALL CALL FOR YOUR DERISION.
Bedford paper

FOR SALE. A rarely comfortable modern detached residence.
Irish Times

Quiet, clean gentleman seeks comfortable room where he can cook himself on a spirit stove.

Münchner Neuste Nachrichten

FOR SALE — Cottage piano made in Berlin, owner getting grand.

Ad in The Pioneer

March 22nd: 'For Sale. Slightly used farm wench in good condition. Very handy. Phone 366-E-2. A. Cartright.'

March 29th: 'Correction. Due to an unfortunate error, Mr. Cartright's ad. last week was not clear. He has an excellent winch for sale. We trust this will put an end to jokesters who have called Mr. Cartright and greatly bothered his housekeeper, Mrs. Hargreaves, who loves with him.

April 9th: 'Notice! My WINCH is not for sale. I put a sledgehammer to it. Don't bother calling 366-R-2. I had the phone taken out. I am NOT carrying on with Mrs. Hargreaves. She merely LIVES here. A. Cartright.

Connecticut paper quoted in Reader's Digest

IF YOU SHOOT YOURSELF AND HAVE NOT USED BLANK'S AMMUNITION, YOU HAVE MISSED ONE OF THE PLEASURES OF LIFE.

Ad in Birmingham paper

ROMANY CARAVAN for sale. Built 1953, sleeps two, ideal bachelor home.

House and Home

FINE WINES AND CIGARS – including the property of a Gentleman of title and of a Gentleman removed from a Mayfair cellar, etc.

Ad in Sunday paper

FOR SALE – Baker's business, good trade, large oven, present owner been in it seventeen years.

Kent paper

WHY KILL THE WIFE? LET US DO YOUR DIRTY WORK

Laundry leaflet

A REAL BUY – 10 Refrigerated Bodies. Must be sold quick. Call Taunton 4.

Canadian paper

FOR SALE – an absolutely perfect gentleman's bicycle.

Irish paper

FUR COAT, THE PROPERTY OF A
LADY CHAUFFEUR; REAL MINX.
Ad in Sunday paper

PIANO – For immediate disposal, powerful toned upright grand, removed from a lady in difficulties.
Ad in Glasgow Evening News

Five rmd house to let, two recep rms, three bedrms, excellent kitchen, separate baths and lavs. (three miles out), 15 minute bus service.
Ad in Northern paper

The book contains a portrait of the author and several other quaint illustrations.
Liverpool paper

FOR SALE — A QUILTED HIGH
CHAIR THAT CAN BE MADE INTO A
PLAY TABLE, POTTIE CHAIR, ROCKING
HORSE, ICE REFRIGERATOR, SPRING
COAT, SIZE 18, WITH FUR COLLAR.
Ad in North Carolina paper

FOR SALE – A small bungalow containing five estate agents.
Local paper

House and shop for sale; excellent position; tenant under notice to expire end of March.

Welsh paper

Oak bedstead, 3ft. 6in. with wife and wool mattress, new condition, £5 lot.

Provincial paper

One unusual feature is a so-called bachelor's chamber with a private bathroom. The maids' bedrooms and bath are conveniently located and are reached by a private stairway.

Newhaven Journal-Courier

TURKEY CARPET FOR SALE GOOD CONDITION THE PROPERTY OF A LADY TOO LARGE FOR HER ROOMS.

Ad in Scotch Daily

The stove will stand by itself anywhere. It omits neither smoke nor smell.

Newcastle paper

RAINCOATS AT LESS THAN COST PRICE LAST THREE DAYS

Ad in Midlands paper

OUR 'ETERNA' FOUNTAIN-PEN IS A
REVOLTING INVENTION.

> German pamphlet

CLOTHES BRUSH. The genuine pigskin back opens
with a zipper and inside are tweezers, scissors, nail-file,
and a bomb.

> Canadian paper

In reply to your valued enquiry, we enclose
illustrations of Dining Tables of Oak, seating
fourteen people with round legs and twelve people
with square legs, with prices attached.

> The Huntly Express

West End Milliner will make latest fashion hat each
month for 18 months for young well-bred greyhound.

> Ad in daily paper

5-seater car for sale; must sell; chauffeur at the Front' own
body cost over £72. What offers? RECTOR.

> Ad in The Times

Double-action Gothic Harp (by Erard),
suitable for a lady in perfect
conditon.

> Provincial paper

Lady, having spent Christmas with her family,
strongly recommends comfortable homely hotel.

Ad in Sussex paper

DETACHED PRIVATE HOTEL, excellently situated near
Torquay Sea Front. Practically on the level.

Devonshire paper

BUSINESS

MODEL WILLING TO POSE FOR
NUDE ARTIST
Card in shop window

An opportunity occurs in a large and rapidly expanding firm
of floor tile manufacturers and contractors for a representative
to cover the Yorkshire and North Eastern Districts.
Ad in The Guardian

THE LIBRARY WILL BE CLOSED FIVE
MINUTES BEFORE CLOSING TIME.
Notice in Munich Public Library

Maximum prices for all corsets and brassières have
been revised. . . . This order also reduced the
percentage uplift allowed to a manufacturer.
Board of Trade Journal

Wanted – Wet fish or experienced man or woman to take
charge of business.
Ad in Bristol Evening Post

It was agreed that existing counter and writing
supervising officers, both men and women, should
immediately be liable to rotate on posts which had
hitherto been reserved to the other sex.
Morning Post

Wanted – Part-time hotel receptionist and telephone operator (small broad). Apply – Hotel, Nicosia.

The Cyprus Mail

The typists' reproduction equipment is not to be interfered with without the prior permission of the manager

Noticed taped on photocopying machine

WANTED, A1 MALE WAITRESS.
DON'T ANSWER UNLESS QUALIFIED.

Ad in Dallas News

Our directors and leaders look swell in their new sweaters, and in the near future it is hoped that they will be provided with a more complete uniform consisting of pants for the men and skirts for the young ladies.

Vancouver Sun

It is easy to slip on polished lino and the special flooring has been introduced in both saloons with this end in view.

Bournemouth paper

UNDERTAKER'S FAILURE
LET DOWN BY CUSTOMERS

Headlines in Yorks. papers

JACK'S LAUNDRY
LEAVE YOUR CLOTHES HERE,
LADIES, AND SPEND THE
AFTERNOON HAVING A GOOD TIME.

Ad in New Mexico paper

The cost of nude models has shocked the rate-payers of a seaside town. More models are needed by the art college at Bournemouth. And that means an extra £800 on the yearly £2,200 bill for models' fees.

Town Councillor, Harold Heath, who is a chairman of Bournemouth's Federation of Ratepayers, said last night: '£800 is a lot of money . . . I think expenditure of this sort should be cut to the bare minimum.'

Daily Mirror

FOREMAN WANTED, TO TAKE
CHARGE OF FEMALES,
SANDPAPERING TURNED LEGS.

Ad in Bury Free Press

Their impression of Gordon's distillery? Cleanliness and efficiency were the two things that particularly impressed them, they told me. They were also very taken with the obvious happiness of the employees.

Morning Advertiser

AN OPPORTUNITY WILL SHORTLY BE
AVAILABLE FOR A SECRETARY OF
IMPEACHABLE CHARACTER, IN A
SMALL OFFICE, OF A NEW INDUSTRY
SHORTLY OPENING NEAR REDRUTH.

West Briton

ONCE YOU HAVE DEALT WITH US YOU WILL RECOMMEND OTHERS.

Ad in East Kent Mercury

EARS PIERCED WHILST YOU WAIT

Notice in Somerset jeweller's shop

WANTED

Some additional female technicians at the fast-expanding
Charles River Breeding Laboratory. No previous
experience necessary.

Ad in Massachusetts paper

Glamour photographer with own equipment and good
contacts seeks sleeping or active partner.

Ad in The Stage

Seventy-one-year-old Mr Dearing, a bachelor, of Station Road, Staines, worked for 20 years as a production controller, and two years as sub-contracting manager. He was presented with his 41st clock by Mr Edward Snell, the boring shop superintendent.

Slough Observer

CUSTOMERS GIVING ORDERS WILL BE PROMPTLY EXECUTED

Notice in Bombay tailor's

HAIRCUTTING WHILE YOU WAIT

Notice in Dublin barber's

Errors. No responsibility can be accepted for losses arising from typographical errors. Advertisers are expected to check their smalls to ensure correct appearance.

Rhodesia Herald

COPY TYPISTS REQUIRE WORK AT HOME. ANTYING AWFUL CONSIDERED.

Rochdale Observer

The strike leaders had called a meeting that was to have been held in a bra near the factory, but it was found to be too small to hold them all.

South London Press

Just out. Revised and enlarged Rules of Punction. A valuable, easy-to-understand text for secretaries, writers, and students. For a free copy send a stamped self-addressed envelope. Ask for Punciation pamphlet.

Indiana paper

The tendency of merchandise offices to restrict buying generally has found some stores very short of corsets – a department which consistently maintained figures throughout the past months.

Draper's Record

GIRL WANTED FOR PETROL PUMP ATTENDANT.

Ad in Oxford Mail

For a limited time, Walkers Ltd. extends the opportunity for business women to take advantage of our professional golf instructor at nominal fees.

Ad in Los Angeles paper

Para. 27b. Men employed on quasi-clerical nature should not be provided with any clothing.

Post Office Magazine

Before placing your orders in the usual channel for the coming term, we should like you to be thoroughly convinced that our services can be dispensed with advantageously.

Tradesman's Circular

THE MILLINERY DEPARTMENT WILL BE ON THE SECOND FLOOR AND THE PROPRIETOR STATES THAT THEIR AIM WILL BE TO ALWAYS HAVE THE LATEST AND LAST WORD IN WOMEN'S HATS AT APPALLING PRICES.

Union City Times, Indiana

I did not see Mr. M— at the Antique Dealer's Fair last week, and later I heard that he has retired from the business and is faking things quietly at home.

Gossip Column

WANTED, SMART YOUNG MAN FOR BUTCHERS. ABLE TO CUT, SKEWER, AND SERVE A CUSTOMER.

Ad in local paper

**GREAT SHOE OFFER . . . EVERY PAIN
GUARANTEED.**

Provincial paper

BUSINESS

Gentleman required, knowledge of shorthand essential although not absolutely necessary.

Essex paper

WANTED, young lady for cutting-up.

Surrey paper

WE DO NOT TEAR YOUR CLOTHES
WITH MACHINERY
WE DO IT CAREFULLY BY HAND

Sign in laundry window

CAPITALIST will consider financing Canadian oil fields or will send English theologist to investigate property.

Ad in daily paper

WRECKER SERVICE–
MEMBER'S CAR WILL BE PULLED OUT OF
DITCH, OR STUCK IN MUD, OR INVOLVED IN
ACCIDENT FREE OF CHARGE WITHIN
RADIUS OF 10 MILES.

Dallas Automobile Club Notice

Strong Boy or Youth wanted for mating on motor lorry.

Ad in Birmingham Gazette

WANTED, Solicitor, experienced in laundry or dye works, to drive wagon.

Vancouver World

THE POST OFFICE DEPARTMENT HAS
ANNOUNCED THAT WHILE THERE
WILL BE NO REGULAR MAIL
DELIVERY ON THANKSGIVING DAY,
A SKELETON WILL MAINTAIN
SERVICE FOR SPECIAL DELIVERY
AND PERISHABLE MATERIAL.

Parkersburg (Virginia) News

WANTED, Man, Military Unfit, to drive van and help hide warehouse.

Canadian paper

Couple, expecting September, require house, flat, furnished, unfurnished, so babe may live in manner to which has been accustomed.

Courier Mail, Brisbane

NOTE TO EMPLOYER
It is regretted that it was not possible to send the enclosed forms to you before the date by which, had you received them in time, you would be required to forward completed copies to the local Employment Exchange.

Ministry of Labour form

C. E. COX BEGS TO ANNOUNCE
THAT HE IS NOW PREPARED TO
DRILL WELLS FOR WATER, GAS, OIL,
CASH OR OLD CLOTHES.

Red Deer Advocate

SAN FRANCISCO (UP) – Edward L. Hayes of Oakland, California, asked the Superior Court today to change his name legally to Tharnmidsbe L. Praghustaponifcem. He said he wanted the change made for 'business and economic reasons'.

The Boston Traveller

MEN REQUIRED BY EXPANDING CONTRACTING COMPANY

Telegraph, Brisbane

BATHS, HOT AND COLD
Under the personal
supervision of the
proprietor.

Hotel advertisement

GIRL wanted as barmaid; bust be attractive.

Seattle Post-Intelligence

WANTED – up-to-date Gas Cooker suitable for bachelor girl with enamelled sides.

Yorks. paper

OUR MOTTO IS TO GIVE OUR
CUSTOMERS THE LOWEST PRICES
AND WORKMANSHIP.

Sign at dry cleaners

Dear madam
With reference to your blue raincoat, our manufacturers have given the garment in question a thorough testing, and find that it is absolutely waterproof. If you will wear it on a dry day, and then take it off and examine it you will see that our statement is correct.
Your obedient servants,

Blank & Co., Drapers

WANTED – 2 women to learn reproduction business; must be strong; good pay to start, with increase as soon as able to produce.

Ad in Boston Globe

```
To taking up floor to find rat and
replacing same . . . 5s. 6d.
```
Builder's invoice

Applications from bona-fide journalists, whether news-paper men* or press photographers, will be welcome.
*Under the rules, man embraces woman.

Ad in trade paper

The Inner Temple Library will be closed during the month of August. Members are notified that they may use the Middle Temple Library.
The Middle Temple Library, in view of extensive repairs, will be closed from 31st July to 30th September inclusive.

Legal paper

HOT WATER ENGINEER, WELL UP COPPER PIPE, DESIRES CHANGE.

Ad in Manchester paper

An official of the Patent Office said that many inventors abandon their parents during their first year of life.

Surrey paper

Chauffeur-handyman, aged 40; wife Vienna cook; occasionally one child.

Ad in Morning paper

The entire estate, totalling nearly £300,000 has been left for the purpose of building a home for indignant people.

Calgary Albertan

B—— & SONS, HOME-DECORATORS
AND PLUMBERS, ETC. ALL WORK
CHEAPLY AND NEARLY DONE.

Ad in Perthshire paper

The Plumbers have finished their part of the contract at the township, and there now remains only the plumbing to be done.

Australian paper

Why rend your garments elsewhere when our up-to-date laundry can do the work more effectively?

New Zealand paper

IRATE HOUSEHOLDERS – WHY BE SWINDLED INA CLUMSY MANNER? FETCH YOUR SECOND-HAND CLOTHING TO ME AND BE DONE IN THE MOST APPROVED STYLE.

Ad in daily paper

Mrs.-- requires useful ladies' maid for town and country; only ex-soldier or sailor need apply.

Provincial paper

OUR LOW PRICES ARE THE DIRECT
RESULT OF OUR LOWERED PRICE POLICY

Ad in New York Times

During the morning there was a steady demand for coarse yarns.

Financial column

NO ICE SOLD AFTER 4 P.M.
ESPECIALLY 5 CENT PIECES

Shop sign in Baltimore

All our season's Goods will be offered at most treasonable prices

Ad in New Zealand paper

We never allow a dissatisfied customer to leave the premises if we can avoid it. It doesn't pay.

Drapery ad in Scottish paper

Americans are offered perfect Grandfathers, one dwarf, one inlaid.

The Connoisseur

TRY OUR PATENT MOSQUITO COIL. IT
IS PERFECTLY SAFE FOR
MOSQUITOES.

Ad in Burmese paper

WANTED FOR LOW COMEDIAN, REALLY FUNNY SONS.

The Stage

Mr.— held that purchased meat should be better than that supplied by contractors, who were not saints. He knew of one case where cattle were actually killed after they died.

Irish Times

WANTED – A steady young woman to wash, iron, and milk two cows.

New Zealand paper

Keen educated young woman wants Agriculture or part Agriculture and Secretarial work in Blandford area. Three months' farm experience, good shorthorn typist.

Ad in West Country paper

Mr Hammond said he would guess the cost of installing the new shunt in each substation between New York and Washington would be between $35,000 and $50,000 and that the world could start in two weeks and be completed in 16 to 20 weeks.

The New York Times

By going on one of our luxury cruises you will shorten the depressing winter months for others as well as yourself.

Shipping company's leaflet

HAND YOUR LUGGAGE TO US
WE WILL SEND IT IN ALL
DIRECTIONS

Ad of Tokyo forwarding agency

Strikebound holidaymakers were kept waiting six hours for the jerry. Then it was filled to capacity.

Southern Echo

In a recent report of a competition held at one of Pontin's holiday camps it was inadvertently stated that it was for 'elephant' grandmothers instead of elegant grandmothers. We apologize to mrs Helen P—, who gained the third place, for any embarrassment this may have caused.

Stockport Advertiser

**CAUTION
THIS HOTEL IS FULLY
LICENSED AND SITUATED ON
THE EAST CLIFF.**

Bournemouth hotel brochure

London Bridge passengers change at Streatham except those marked with an asterisk.

Time table

Britain's latest and most up-to-date atom power station has as its centre-piece a unique giant steel sphere 135 feet in diameter, constructed to house a fast-breeding rector.

Cyprus Mail

METAPHORS

IT MUST BE TRUE

WE MIGHT QUOTE YOU EXTRACTS
FROM OUR ROOMFUL OF
UNSOLICITED TESTIMONIALS, BUT
AN OUNCE OF FACT IS WORTH A TON
OF FICTION.

From a circular

Tom and I are like blood brothers. He means more to me than my own flesh and Mrs Denise Baines of Balaclava Road, Cambridge.

Cambridge News

It is the new magistrates who have broken the ice, and the supporters of both camps are curiously watching to see if they will find themselves in hot water.

Liverpool Echo

Dr. Barrett says these lawyers are so thin that it is possible to see vertically through them and that makes them invisible from the ground, except at sunrise or sunset on clear days.

Montreal Star

One on the outside who criticises the placement of square pegs in round holes should be sure that there are not more round holes and square pegs than there are square holes and round pegs. Even if this is not the case the critic should be certain that round holes are not a more serious problems than square ones, and he should withhold his criticism unless he is quite sure that it is better to leave round holes unfilled than it is to fill them partially with square pegs.

American Journal of Public Health

In fact, it would almost appear that certain journals of the type under discussion are incapable of keeping their heads above water except by stooping to wash dirty linen in order to tickle the ears of the groundlings.

China Republican

```
He finds himself in a dual position
and may not know through which horn of
the dilemma he could sound his
trumpet.
```

Nigerian paper

It appears to us that Mr. Dewey would have been wielding a double-edged sword in the shape of a boomerang that would have come home to plague him and beat him by a large majority.

Northampton (Mass.) Hampshire Gazette

Let us nip this political monkey business in the bud before it sticks to us like a leech.

Letter in San Francisco Chronicle

Mr. Lloyd George, patron saint of the Liberal Party, was a very astute gentleman with both ears glued firmly to the ground. Naturally he could not see very far ahead.

Scottish paper

This criticism is not open, as Britishers would be, and consequently is difficult to nail down, but, like a snake in the grass, is whispered behind a hand which covers a sneering face.

Letter in Rugeley Mercury

In the first important utterance of the Chairman of the Board, he has, so to say, thrown the Board overboard and ploughed his own canoe.

Ceylonese paper

In addition to the fine work done by the Irish regiments he assured them that many a warm Irish heart beat under a Scottish kilt.

Daily paper

CONCERTS & ENTERTAINMENT

Vocalists who sang the quartet very beautifully were Miss Jackman, Miss Mountford, Mrs. Jackman, and Mr. Palmer; the latter's rendering of 'Honk, Honk, the Lark' was full of charm.

Belfast paper

Old German dances on the harpsichord.

Radio paper

Fugue in E Flat . . . Major Bach

Concert programme

3.30 Church Cantata No. 125, Bach
In Peace and Joy Shall I depart
with Doris Belcher, Contralto

Radio programme

Q. What does the name Lear mean in Shakespeare's King Lear?
A. It is of Celtic origin and means SLEEVE VALVE ENGINE.

Washington Daily News

AUDIENCE TRIED TO SPOIL PLAY BUT ST. CHAD'S PLAYERS SUCCEEDED

Sunderland Echo

During her career as a contralto singer Miss C— has visited many capital cities.

Illustrated paper

Miss Gorman, in a quiet part as a nice woman, makes it obvious that she is a very good actress indeed.

Canadian paper

Another performance of the pantomime is to be given in the Parish Hall, and this will give all those who missed seeing it another chance of doing so.

Sporting paper

THE PROGRAMME WILL FEATURE
COMEDIE FRANCAIS, THE GREAT
FRENCH ACTRESS.

Cinema Ad in Scots paper

Follies Parisienne
See! Nudes in the Waterfall
Daring fan dance. Virgin and the Devil
Sensational dance of the Strip Apache
Les Beaux Mannequins de Parisienne
Continental and Oriental Nudes
Old Age Pensioners Monday

Ad in Leciester paper

Despite a temporary bitch in the opening chorus of the second act, Mr Jones earned high praise for his skilful stage management.

Review of 'The Gondoliers'

This week's hint. When speaking or singing be sure to turn your face to the audience as far as possible. One hundred and twenty first quality eggs should weigh 17 lbs.

From a theatre programme

SATURDAY NIGHT DANCE
VERY EXCLUSIVE
EVERYBODY WELCOME

Notice outside dance hall

Be Thou With Me (Bach)
with Organ accpt.
My Heart Ever Faithful (Bach)
with Orch. accpt.
Art Thou Troubled with the City of
Birmingham Orchestra (Handel).
I'm going to My Naked Bed
(Unaccompanied) – Madrigal.

Concert programme

A Variety Concert was held on Wednesday at St Anthony's Theatre, Merchants' Quay, at 8 pm. The injured were taken to hospital, most of them with second and third degree burns.

Evening Press, Dublin

9.5 SHERLOCK HOLMES AS DR WATSON IN 'STUDY IN SCARLET'.

Ad in Dublin Evening Herald

John F—, the celebrated singer, was in a motor-car accident last week. We are happy to state he was able to appear the following evening in four pieces.

Bradford paper

```
In last night's performance of The
Gondoliers, Mr Robertson, as the Grand
inquisitor, might have been a gentleman
in reality, so ably did he fill the
part.
```

Provincial paper

Under the baton of Mr S. Rutherford the Cosmopolitan Club orchestra provided musical numbers. Miss Maisie Ringell's outstanding features convulsed the audience.

Gisborne Herald

We charge low prices of admission but they are recognised by our regular visitors as being consistent with the quality of the films screened.

Singapore Free Press

WANTED—POSITION IN CABARET; NO BAD HABITS; WILLING TO LEARN.

Boston News

The famous German composer, Karl Maria von Weber, was born in Eutin, Oldenburg, in 1786, a few weeks after the production in Germany, at Covent Garden, of his opera Oberon.

Indiana paper

Miss S— sang the first verse and then the audience all sank together.

Local paper

The programme for today at the Opera compromises Samson et Dalila.

Continental Daily Mail

In printing yesterday the name of one of the musical comedies which the Bandmaster Company is presenting next week as The Grill in the Train, what our compositor meant to set was, of course, The Girl in the Drain.

South China Morning Post

At the studios, a tiny baby was needed for a scene in The Enemy. The call came to Peggy C—, studio nurse. 'Please have a baby by eight o'clock tomorrow morning.'

Photoplay

COME IN YOUR THOUSANDS. THE HALL HOLDS FIVE HUNDRED.

Concert bill

An item which was deservedly appreciated and encored was Chopin's Pollonaise 'Sea Miner'.

Wexford Free Press

It was heard under excellent conditions, Miss Wayne and Mrs Charles were obviously at home and in complete sympathy with their parts, the mooing duet being sung with the deepest feeling and dramatic fervour.

Yorkshire Evening News

Twenty-two members were present at the meeting of the R.L.D.S. Church held at the home of Mrs. Edith Marchfield last evening. Mrs. Ruth Bayliss and Monica Hotton sung a duet, The Lord Knows Why.

Attleboro (Massachusetts) Sun

Before Miss Jenkinson concluded the concert by singing 'I'll walk beside you' she was prevented with a bouquet of red roses.

Sussex paper

Moby Dick, the great American classic by Herman Melville, will be seen again next week with veteran actor Victor Jory in the title role.

Los Angeles News

THE MERRY WIDOW WITH ADDED SHORTS

Cinema placard

ANATOMY AND CLEOPATRA

Bookseller's catalogue

Miss —, who only recently returned from England, is included in an otherwise strong cast.

South African paper

TRY THE LONDON PAVILION,
8.30 P.M. JUST THE THING FOR A
DULL EVENING.

Ad in The Daily News

D-- Amateur Operatic Society. Booing office opens on Monday.

Provincial paper

NEW YORK, March 4th – Helen Hayes, whose work on the stage was interrupted by maternity, is to return in a manless play.

Columbus Dispatch

THIS WILL BE A SHOW WHICH YOU MUST NOT FAIL TO MISS.

Ad in Rangoon paper

The Ballet travels with its own symphony orchestra which is directed by Mrs. Golberman. The orchestra contains 20 virtuous performers.

Clemson College Tiger

THE BIBLICAL STORY, BASED ON A LIBRETTO BY OSCAR WILDE, RECOUNTS THAT . . .

Associated Press Dispatch

The Concert held in the Good Templar's Hall was a great success . . . Special thanks are due to the Vicar's daughter, who laboured the whole evening at the piano, which as usual fell upon her.

South African paper

Miss T-- sang a number of popular
ballads while the orchestra played some
Strauss waltzes.

Parish magazine

IT'S THEIR SHOW – Mr. and Mrs. Alvan W.
Sulloway, of Concord, N.H., librettist and composer
of 'Winner Take All'. She writes music with her
three little boys on her hands.

Boston Globe

On Wednesday evening Mr. R— proposes to take the life
of one of the modern poets.

Durham paper

Before sailing for Egypt, John spent a few days in
Dorset and no doubt then wrote the verses entitled:
'Somewhere in England' and beginning:
EFFECTS OF RHEUMATISM

Dorset County Chronicle

LOCAL GOVERNMENT & POLITICS

The Post Office sought permission to erect telephone poles on the Llanfoist housing site. They have been told that whilst the Council do not object to the installation of telephones, they consider the poles should be laid underground.

Abergavenny Chronicle

It has usually been the custom to get some prominent gentleman to take the chair, but on this occasion the selection fell on Councillor Eastland.

Bristol paper

The service director said that the city had neither the money nor the equipment to restore the brides; they had deteriorated rapidly and were in need of extensive repairs.

Tiffin (Ohio) Tribune

'This budget leakage is something that's got to stop,' said the President, with what seemed to be more than a trace of irrigation in his voice.

Jackson (Missouri) State Times

BRAVO PORTHCAWL! IT IS SOMETHING TO BE PROUD OF TO HAVE THE LOWEST INFANTILE MORALITY IN THE KINGDOM.

Welsh paper

I made no promises to perform impossibilities as I have found in practice that these are very seldom carried out.

Election candidate's letter

FARR, EDWARD — SELECTED
POULTRY, CHIEFLY DEVOTIONAL, OF
THE REIGN OF QUEEN ELIZABETH.

Book catalogue

The Mayor-Elect presided, and to him fell the duty of proposing the death of the Mayor, which he did in felicitous terms.

Local paper

A proposal of the Harrisburg Redevelopment Authority involving possible demolition of the city's new planner when he takes office next Friday, it was indicated yesterday.

Harrisburg (Pennsylvania) Patriot

'The lack of toilet facilities is absolutely disgraceful,' he said. The only solution was a major reconstruction of the House or a new Chamber.

The Daily Telegraph

Londonderry Development Commission has plans to spend about £24,000 within the next few months on improving the standard of street fighting in the city centre and a number of housing estates.

Belfast Telegraph

Several eligible sires for workmen's dwellings, have been selected by the Southport Town Planning Committee.

Daily paper

COUNCIL 'DIGGING OWN GRAVE' SMALLER BODY URGED

Ottawa Citizen

At Caxton Hall the conference was resumed of Municipal authorities interested in the conversation of old fruit, sardine, and salmon tins.

Birmingham Daily Mail

. . . but the petition of Stanley Zwier, American civic worker, who was found this morning shoved under the door of the City Manager's officer, will be accepted.

New Jersey paper

The Hon. Treasurer (Mr. Hodgson) stated that he was willing to carry on in his office until he had to move from the town, which might be at any time (applause).

Andover Advertiser

We had argued and weighed the merits of the candidates, and most of us were now for Eisenhower. But suddenly we became concerned. 'Can Eisenhowe strike its mark unless the shaft is as usual, a batch of filmy underthings hooked in one elbow.
'I washed your things,' he announced. And I knew at last that I was dreaming.

Herald Tribune

ARRIVAL IN BOMBAY OF LORD
WILLINGDON THE NEW GOVERNOR
AND DEPARTURE OF LORD
SYDENHAM AND THREE OTHER
COMICS

News cinema ad

WASHINGTON— Nov. 23 (INS). Price Administrator Bowles told the Senate Small Business committee yesterday that sugar rationing cannot be lifted unless domestic production is increased very greatly and that the increase of production rests with War Food Administrator Jones, and four grandchildren.

St Louis Star Times

The Churchillian jaw was out-thrust and the Prime Minister thumped the despatch box with a heavy fish.

Canadian paper

BRITAIN'S PART IN PEOPLING THE COMMONWEALTH ROLE OF 'SLEEPING PARTNER' NOT ENOUGH.

Manchester Guardian

In the past the Council had felt that the first thing they should do was to get the storm water out of the sewers before trying to force home-owners in. It was decided at last night's meeting that where the sewers could take the waste water without flooding, the owners should be told to get in now.

Bryan (Ohio) Times

A Council of Action has been set up. This decided yesterday not to take any immediate action.

Bucks paper

Thank God we have a Prime Minister who does not always wait to cross a bridge until he comes to it.

Letter in The Times

THE CHANCELLOR OF THE EXCHEQUER WILL SPEAK AT 5 P.M. BEWARE OF PICKPOCKETS

Notice at Conservative garden party

With reference to the comments on certain members of the Provincial Assembly, contained in our issue of two days ago, we beg our readers to note that the expressions used were not intended to possess their ordinary meaning.

Chinese paper

The Lord Mayor, in reply, said: 'I rise to respond to the toast of the Lord Mayor and the Sheriffs of the City of London, so charmingly proposed by Mrs. Harrison. There would appear to be hardly any limit to the activities of that ancient body.'

Surrey paper

For some weeks now this method has been tried out at the Guildhall by members of the County Council staff. It is now considered foolproof.

Evening paper

Alderman S— said the Council ought to be given the whole truth that there was still sufficient coal in the city to last five weeks if nobody used it.

Yorkshire paper

Councillor B— said he was worried about the town's fuel supply. When the previous Council had been in office the output of gas had been considerable.

Yorkshire paper

The Sanitary Surveyor reported that he had been able to obtain six bottles of rat poison, and that he was sending a bottle to the Chairman of the S— Parish Council.

Devon paper

CAN CIVILISATION SURVIVE? WITH A.M. PALMER M.P. IN THE CHAIR.

Handbill

HAMPSTEAD BOROUGH
CORPORATION
SO NOT SPIT AROUND THIS
SEAT

Notice board

Labourers and dockers, men working on buses and the railway, glassblowers, stevedores, caretakers, schoolmasters, and even the criminal classes – such as local doctors and solicitors – can be found on its books.

Appeal for Working Men's Club

Following on yesterday's defeat of the Government in the Dail, a meeting of the Cabinet was hell this morning.

Dublin paper

Along the Parkway, schoolchildren hurled roses in the General's path. Two schoolgirls presented him with a large bouquet of roses. 'God bless you, my children, and thank you,' he said as he killed both girls.

Philadelphia paper

There is one such building now being erected within a few miles of Manchester as the cock crows.

Manchester paper

Madrid proposes to utilize the water brought to the city by an old camel to produce about three thousand electrical horse power.

Montreal Gazette

Three hundred emigrants arrived here today by train 90 per cent of them being people of both sexes.

Irish paper

PASSENGERS HIT BY CANCELLED TRAINS

Manchester Evening News

MILITARY

The marksmanship of the headquarters company is highly satisfactory and the shooting of the regimental sergeant-major was especially praiseworthy.

Daily Express

It is necessary for technical reasons that these warheads should be stored with the top at the bottom, and the bottom at the top. In order that there may be no doubt as to which is the top and which is the bottom for storage purposes, it will be seen that the bottom of each head has been plainly labelled with the word TOP.

Admiralty instruction

It is proposed to use this donation for the purchase of new wenches for our park as the present ones are in a very dilapidated state.

Carrolton (Ohio) Chronicle

FIFTH ARMY SEIZES JUNCTION OF PARALLEL ROADS TO ROME.

Washington News

The President of the Board of Trade has appointed a Committee to consider the important question of employment for soldiers and sailors in the war.

Daily Telegraph

Smoking is allowed so long as it does not interfere with the work, but when the D.S.O. or any senior officers approach the station it would be as well if they were removed for the time being.

Territorial instruction

Scandinavia has no doubt that in the latter half of last week a naval engagement took place between Great Britain and Germany in the North Sea. The evidence is that of kippers who, using their eyes and ears, put two and two together.

The Star

Lieut. and Mrs. James A. W—- announce the birth of a son, James Allen, at James Connally Air Base, Waco, Texas. He will report for duty at Langley Air Base, Virginia, next Sept. 9.

Greensboro (N. Carolina) Record

A resolution was passed which instructed Secretary Rigg to write to the department of militia asking for (a) the names of the shoe-makers who were catering for the feeding of the troops, (b) the names of the cooks and caterers supplying the boots and shoes.

Winnipeg Free Press

TOMORROW (SUNDAY) — CHURCH
PARADE. 'FALL IN' AT BARNES
POND, 10 A.M. (WITHOUT RIFLES).

Barnes and Mortlake Herald

I am sending you my marriage certificate and six children there were seven but one died You only sent six back, her name was fanny and was baptised on a half sheet of paper by the reverend Thomas.

Letter received by Army Pay Office

LEAVE REGULATIONS – Section 2. When an employee absent from duty on account of illness dies without making application for sick leave, the fact of death is sufficient to show a 'serious disability' and to dispense with the requirement of a formal application and a medical certificate.

U.S. Government order

Officers, they say, should be selected from those whose intelligence, as measured by tests, reaches a cretain value.

Scottish paper

British gumboots have been compelled to reply to attacks upon them from the banks of the Yangtse-Kiang river.

New Zealand paper

The excavations started in North Africa in 1939 were interrupted by the war. The war was sponsored by the American School of Prehistoric Research.

Boston Herald

TO BRING WIVES OVER BY TELEPHONE WITHOUT PERMITS, CONSULT MR.——, MARINE SUPERINTENDENT AND RECEIVER OF WRECKS.

Notice of naval base

PROMOTION. Rifleman P. R. Shand to be Sergeant H. Cock.

Ceylon paper

Tomorrow week the Canadian regimental doctors will be deposited for safe keeping in Bristol Cathedral.

Bristol paper

Swooping to a few hundred feet, Nazi planes dropped parachutists on to a narrow plateau, then climbed over a 10ft. wall, and there was Mussolini at an upstairs window.

Belfast paper

LOOKING FOR THAT SILVER LINING?

You'll find it for sure with the U.S. Army. At no expense, you'll get the finest medical and dental scare.

American paper

It is up to the regular establishments to institute training programmes that will result in a constant weeding out of those who are found unwilling to or incapable of becoming incompetent.

American government circular

WORLD PEACE, NOW AS NEVER BEFORE, DEPENDS FOR ITS PRESERVATION UPON THEM ASSES.

Daily paper

The total number of prisoners captured by us in this sector is not yet available. We secured Mayoress, Mrs. Hogg, Mrs. R. Nay, Miss South of the Scarpe.

Provincial paper

In 1918 he was appointed business manager of the Great War at a salary of £15 per week.

West Country paper

EDUCATION

Ladies who have kindly undertaken to act as school crossing wardens are reminded again that if they attempt to carry out their duties without their clothing on motorists are unlikely to take notice of them.

> Circular to school parents

MEDINA TO HAVE PARENT TEACHER ASSASSINATION

> Headline in Medina (Oregon) Sentinel

Student behaviour at Essex University, Colchester, 'makes Lady Chatterly's Lover like a vicarage tea party!' in comparison, Mr George Milsom, county councillor, said yesterday. Essex County Council agreed to cut their annual £107,000 grant by £1.

> Daily Mail

'In the sixth form we've been trying to get uniform done away with. I think we'll soon be down to the boys just wearing a tie and the girls a grey skirt.'

> Daily Mail

Mr E. G. Winterton, headmaster, would not comment on the threat. However, he did say: 'Some children have been behaving very childishly'.

> Doncaster Post

For his comfort the roadman has a brassière which is very nice on a cold day.

Schoolgirl's Essay

Word was received last week that Mrs Gertrude Higgins, teacher of the 36th Street School, was severely bitten by a dog on the school grounds. Principal Gail Mahoney observed that it could just as easily have been a child.

Los Angeles South-West News-Press

As for this puzzler: 'Was it he you were talking to' or 'Was it him you were talking to', Mr Lewis says the correct sentence would be: 'Was it he to whom you can also say it was she I were talking'. However, he adds, was thinking about.

Pittsburgh Press

Letters were sent to 665 men. Each envelope was marked 'Important' in large letters, so that those men who could not read might ask to have the letters read to them.

American Education Digest

FRIENDS' ACADEMY, LOCUST VALLEY, LONG ISLAND, CO-EDUCATIONAL, WITH SPECIAL OPPORTUNITIES FOR BOYS.

Friend's Intelligencer

P —— MANOR SCHOOL
HIGH-CLASS HOME SCHOOL
FOR GIRLS
EXAMINATION SUCCESSES QUITE
EXCEPTIONAL

Ad in Manchester Courier

Although a large number of children partake of free meals at the school canteens, the proportion found to be suffering from marked malnutrition is a modest one.

Kent paper

Formerly a don at Oxford, he developed later an interest in education, and migrated to Ontario.

Canadian Review

GREAT SERVICE TO EDUCATION
Mr. Eric Jones Resigns From
County Committee

Salisbury Journal

Please excuse John from school today as father's ill and the pig has to be fed.

Letter to Schoolmaster

His wife too is beginning to learn the language, and the twins, are eagerly awaiting to start school. They speak only German, but already know how to say 'kindergarten'.

Deluth News-Tribune

The macaw of British Honduras says a lecturer resembles many people in wearing fine clothes, making a great noise, and in being good for nothing else.

Evening News

Mrs. Thomas J—'s classes for children of pre-kindergarten age will be resumed on Mondays, Wednesdays and Fridays, from 9 to 12 o'clock. A slight smack will be served at 10.30.

Connecticut paper

DAVID B. WALKER JOINS STAFF TO TEACH JUVENILE DELINQUENCY

Adult Education Newsletter

Students who marry during their course will not be permitted to remain in college. Further, students who are already married must either live with their husbands or make other arrangements with the dean.

Syllabus of an Ohio College

Mme Albani, it is announced, is going to take a limited number of pupils, but has been sunk. The crew were saved.

North Western Daily Mail

P. T. Harris gained credit for himself and for Wellingborough Grammar School by passing in every subject and gaining four distinctions – in arithmetic, French, algebra and Little Bowden Pig Club.

Market Harborough Advertiser

A party from the Grammar School, Ilkeston, of nineteen girls, fourteen boys, two mistresses of one master, leave for an eight days' tour of Paris.

The Ilkeston Pioneer

After many years persecution, and twelve children, Mrs. Leah Elkin, Brooklyn, finally graduated from high school.

Kansas City Star

WORDS OFTEN MISUSED: Do not say: 'We then drove over the bride.' Say: 'We then drove across the bride.'

Union City Hudson Dispatch

```
The Librarian reports that we now have
in our Reference Library a larger
number of boobs than has any other
library in the County.
```

West Country Library

SAY IT RIGHT
Today's names in the news and how to pronounce them:
Syngman Rhee, President of Korea; pronounced Sung-mahn Ree.
Jacques Fath, French fashion designer; pronounced Ellsa Skee-ah-pah-rell-ee.

Miami Daily News

GARDENING

Order your nuts now. If you have any difficulty, drop me an envelope addressed to yourself and marked 'Nuts'.

Gardening column in Reveille

Miss Hazel Foster's gladioli garden has been attracting considerable attention of late. She spends many hours among her large collection of pants.

Pennsylvania paper

Chestnut fencing and garden screening. Illustrated cat on request.

Gardening weekly

WANTED — GARDENER; MUST BE
EXPERIENCED, OR USELESS.

Ad in Wilts paper

Southampton Flower Show was found by a mushroom picker in the Ettlingen Forest, near Karlsruhe, Germany. It had drifted 470 miles.

Yorkshire Evening Press

OFFICIAL ADVICE—Don't grow your potatoes where they will not grow.

Daily Express

Nothing brightens the garden in spring more than primrose pants.

Weekly paper

5. Q. What is the origin of the word 'Miami'?
A. From the French spelling of the Indian word 'Maumee', meaning 'Miami'.

Florida grower

I am very pleased with the lot of seeds I got from you recently. Every one nearly came up.

Testimonial in Seedsman's catalogue

Here is a genuine offer of finest quality guaranteed flowering-size bulbs at prices having no relation to their real worth.

Ad in gardening paper

About a month ago a long red radish reached us from a reader the normal size of a carrot.

Amateur Gardening

I once got a circular from a man who grew potatoes containing his photograph and, I think, an autobiography.

Musical Standard

Gardeners should waste no time. Tie your pants in now before the south-easters blow.

Ad in Cape Town paper

For such seeds there is no need to draw drills. They are best scattered on the surface and then lightly raked in with the tips of the teeth.

Suffolk paper

GARDENING

Our picture shows Mr. Robert Tenter rolling the lawn with his fiancée, Miss Elizabeth Briarcliffe.

Bucks. paper

Dig the ground over thoroughly and then pant.

Gardening article

Practise thinning in winter time and head back in summer. A tree can be kept bearing practically regular crops. Of course it is impossible to keep any tree bearing practically regular crops, but of course it is impossible to keep any tree bearing a full crop regularly. Wonders can be done by this system of pruning.

Nurseryman's leaflet

LOVE & ROMANCE

Deryk stood watching her, his hands in his pockets, a splendid specimen of English manhood in his white flannels, his tennis racket in his strong brown hands.

Story in church paper

The door opened and a girl came in – a slip of a girl with a firm little chin and a pair of lively grey ewes which gave Bernard a searching glance.

Australian paper

Wanted, companion for two ladies in bath (Som.)

The Lady

'Today', she said, and he held up his thumb and grinned at her. If only this could be for ever, the two of them alone. But the sea lifted the boat like a sullen cork, and he stopped thinking about anything but handling her.

John Bull

He told Mrs X he had a record of the complete works of the Messiah and she arranged to visit his house the next day to hear it.

'I was playing the Messiah for about 10 minutes when she said this was not the right occasion for such music,' he went on. 'She started to make overtures to me.'

News of the World

For her birthday he gave her a lunch of tulips and daffodils.

ABC film review

Gentleman desires genuine friendship of unattached lady, 40–45, any reply answered confidently.

Reading Chronicle

If you're in a cinema, put your arm round her and don't be bashful. All the people around you are doing the same.

Letter in Sunday Pictorial

Young men are beginning to object tousle-headed girls in ill-made, mannish clothes. Girls, it seems to me, are not especially pleased with unshaven, uncouth, ungallant boys or varicose ulcer.

Philadelphia Enquirer

My wife is passionately fond of flowers, and I always give her a punch on her birthday.

Letter in daily paper

She raised her head, startled, and stared at a young boy who was smiling at her. Spread around her was a sun-flooded valley where buttercups nodded lazily in the summer breeze and tranquil cows chewed solemnly at her elbow.

Western Family Magazine

When a Suffolk fisher-lad sets his heart upon a maiden, he does not beat about the bust.

Adelaide Register

Again for an instant she raised those wonderful eyes to his. He studied the thickness of the lashes as they fell once more to her lap.

Truth

For what lad can behold a pretty girl weeping for him without drying her ears on his breast.

Dorothy Dix in the Boston Globe

WANTED — YOUNG MAN WOULD
LIKE TO MEET YOUNG LADY
WITH 2 BOXES OF 12 GAUGE
SHOTGUN SHELLS. OBJECT
MATRIMONY. WRITE M.M. IN CASE
OF THIS OFFICE.

Wisconsin paper

He looked at her with infinite tenderness. 'I know all about it,' he said.
She covered her face with her hands and cried brokenly. But, coming closer, he put both hands on her shoulders, and lifted her tea-stained face to his.

Tasmanian Courier Annual

'I – I didn't know you care for me in that way. I've always thought of you as just a great big bother.'

Newspaper Serial

'I've something to tell you, Peggy. I may call you Piggy, mayn't I?'

Short story

He leaned his head against her hair. A wasp strayed across his face. He kissed it.

Novelette

Mary's eyes rested lovingly on the little gold brooch. 'Oh, Jack,' she murmured, 'it's the loveliest gilt I've ever had.'

Serial story

The last he saw of her was as she turned out of a side-street into the main road, tearing up the latter as she went.

Weekly paper

He was asked if he contemplated any further act of matrimony.
'Certainly' was his evasive reply.

New York World

'Yes,' she said, 'those things over there are my husbands.'

Newspaper serial

Lady wishes to exchange from 15th July to 15th September, young Englishman for young Frenchman.

Daily paper

SPORT

The fox made a bee-line through the Hall grounds, then on through the village, to the delight of the hundreds of spectators. Scent was lost in the fields that skirt the south side of the village, but a few moments later there were shouts in a garden near to the church, and within a few minutes the hounds had killed these scores of sightseers looking on from the surrounding gardens. It was one of the most exciting days we can remember.

Wilts. paper

```
Channel swim attempt
Boston girl's arrival in Liverpool
```
Liverpool Echo

It was a sort of Daniel and Goliath battle, in which the stronger and bigger man always appeared to hold the mastery.

Scottish paper

Resisting the temptation to shoot himself at close range, he cleverly flicked the ball sideways to Humphries.

The Times

Dr S— is associated with societies for the prohibition of cruel sports, recorder playing and Welsh folk songs.

Yorkshire Post

Our picture shows the Berlin Bowling Club team which won the Ladies' Fencing Contest for Austria.

Caption in illustrated paper

As the four finalists hit the last bend, he produced an electrifying bust which swept him past his opponents into the home straight to breast the tape.

Carmarthen Journal

```
I know boys will be boys, and I am not
opposed to a modicum of high spirits
after a successful match, but when it
comes to scattering tintacks on the
changing room floor, as your trainer I
must really put my food down.
```

From a Norfolk football club bulletin

Wooden benches for the crucial fourth India–Australia Test in Calcutta have been replaced by cricket officials.

Daily Express

Preston went to Craven Cottage encouraged by three successive away wins. They finished up adding another triumph at the expense of a team considered invisible at home.

Sunday Post

Walter Hornbaker, South Fayette St, bagged a 4-point buck, Robert Thomas, RRI, bagged a 6-point buck, and Billy Dovey of Loudon Rd.

Mercersburg (Pennsylvania) Journal

Four riders cleared the course of about 800 yards with 14 obstacles, including Miss Richardson (Britain) on Cobler.

Scottish Sunday Express

Six minutes later Blackpool went further ahead, when Matthews saw his left foot curl into the net off a post.

Football report

At the start of the race Yale went out in front, rowing at a terrific clip above 40. It had half a mile lead after the first quarter mile.

New York Times

The thing that first caught my eye was a large silver cup that Charles had won for skating on the mantelpiece.

Short story

The last wicket fell just before lunchtime. After the interval a very pleasing improvement in the dimensions of the spectators was seen.

East Anglian Daily Times

The accuracy of the England bowling was shown by the fact that R— was at the wicket for twenty minutes before snoring.

Evening paper

SATURDAY'S FOOTBALL
POOWONG 40 GALS 39 BEHINDS
Great Southerner Advocate, Victoria

It is estimated that about 16 foxes were shot or killed by the hounds.

Peninsula Post

In the current number of golfing weekly, J. H. Taylor gives a description of the early days at Westward Ho! Golf was then played in a state of nature.

Pall Mall Gazette

Hampshire elected to bath first on a pitch damp on top from the early morning rain.

Wolverhampton Express and Star

DUCHESS TO RACE GREYHOUNDS

Northampton paper

Miss Polly R—, the home centre-forward, was continually bursting down the middle.

Yorkshire Post

With nine wickets down, Enthoven changed his tactics and bit both bowlers.

Manchester paper

So the engineers staged an endurance run. The drivers worked in three 8-hour shifts, the cars stopping only long enough to be checked, refuelled and their drivers hanged.

Corpus Christi (Texas) paper

M— L—, who toured with the All Blacks, at the match on Saturday last kicked three gals in succession.

New Zealand paper

TODAY'S GOLF HINT. IF YOUR
DRIVING IS NOT SO GOOD AS USUAL
TRY TO GET THE LEFT HIP AND
CLUBHEAD TO STRIKE THE BALL AT
THE SAME INSTANT.

Provincial paper

On a Winnipeg course golfers – little animals which live underground like rabbits – have become collectors of golf balls. In one of their underground storehouses 250 golf balls were discovered.

Bombay paper

Another resolution gives umpires the power, without reference to the captains, to have the wicked dried during the progress of a match.

Northants paper

Miss Sandiston, who is only 19, has grown since last year. In patches her form is most impressive.

Essex paper

Robinson, who had been auctioned several times by the referee, was ordered off the field.

Sussex paper

That hunting and fishing are good in Colorado is shown by the fact that of 100,000 hunters out during the recent game season there were 80,000 killed. This is a record that cannot be equalled in the United States.

Colorado paper

R— had survived three appeals for l.b.w. before the players retired to lynch.

Daily paper

Round 3.- Both continued to be cautious in the first minuet, but opened up in the second minuet, when both got in good lefts to the head.

Birmingham paper

Edward Slater broke his arm last week. It was a decided success and many expressed the wish that it might be an annual affair.

American paper

In an interview he said: 'I have been all over the world looking for the perfect golf curse, but I think at last I have found it.'

Evening paper

As a matter of fact, Jackson calmly waited to be fetched, and I fear his suffering was not so great as people thought. He dislocated a hip hip hurrah, and was soon all right again.

Provincial paper

Ten sampans were entered, the boats being gaily decorated with flags. The result was a very amusing race in which the winner passed the post only a length behind the second.

Hongkong Overseas Mail

The forwards shot hard and often but never straight till at last Hill decided to try his hand. It came off first time.

Kent paper

'If it is not worth while going on with the race it is not worth while going on with the race it is not worth while going on with the race,' commented Dr. Saleeby.

Manchester Evening Chronicle

DOMESTIC

INSTRUCTIONS
POUR A TEASPOON OF THE SHAMPOO
INTO THE PALM OF EACH HAND . . .

Label on bottle

This summer the Graham family – father, mother and teenage daughter – will move into the bungalow which they have planned and built themselves from books borrowed from their local library.

Sunday Express

Keeping all food under cover is the first step towards ridding the house of aunts.

Albany Journal

Send mother a gift of hardly ever blooming rose bushes.

Sioux Falls Argus-Leader

Dip your soiled face in alcohol, rinse it in the liquid and hang it straight out to dry. It may then be pressed.

Toronto Mail

Wrap poison bottles in sandpaper and fasten with scotch tape or a rubber band. If there are children in the house, lock them in a small metal box.

Philadelphia Record

DOMESTIC

Sprinkle on the shelves a mixture of half borax and half sugar. This will poison every aunt that finds it.

Norwick (Connecticut) Bulletin

Miss June Brown was a week-end guest at the Louis Scholl home. Mrs Louis Scholl was also a guest at the same home.

Ashland (Ohio) Times-Gazette

```
My children are good looking and
healthy and appear to be normal but
they are such little terrors that they
are making my life unbearable. What is
your advice? vice?
```

Waterbury (Connecticut) American

Household hint: Ink can more easily be removed from a white tablecloth before it is spilled than after.

Provincial paper

They have acquired a pleasant country house in Berkshire for they are both lovers of the country, which they are having altered and decorated to their taste.

Theatrical paper

Mrs J. Gearing of Sebring, Florida, is visiting this week in the home of Mrs Melvina Burtis, Mrs Gearing died a few years ago.

Ludlow (Vermont) Tribune

WHY BREAK YOUR CHINA WASHING UP?
DO IT AUTOMATICALLY IN A DISHWASHER!
FROM JOHN R. FORDHAM, EPPING.
'PHONE 33.
ESTABLISHED 1923.

Ad in Surrey Mirror

When the baby is done drinking it must be unscrewed and laid in a cool place under a tap. If the baby does not thrive on fresh milk it should be boiled.

Women's magazine

Lawrence Beal has recovered from a visit to relatives in Newcastle NH and Boston.

Ellsworth (Maine) American

Mrs.— will not be 'at home' to her friends today. PIGS.

Argentine paper

For the past many years I've huffed and puffed when struggling with rubbers and overshoes, both for my plum self and wriggling spaghetti-legged youngster.
No more!
I now put the shoes inside of chicken over certain vegetables. Mushroom soup is the rain boots first then step is good with peas in the shoes. Sure is easier.

Nyack (NY) Journal News

When the wives are bottled they are put into a cool cellar and kept there for some time.

Evening paper

'Put soap on the runners of the bureau drawers instead of jerking them in and out until they fall apart,' advises John Litwinko.

'If that doesn't help, take the the Methodist Episcopal Church.'

Philadelphia Evening Bulletin

To prevent a little girl's hair-slide from constantly slipping, put an elastic band or a piece of bicycle valve tubing round the under arm, opposite the teeth.

Woman's Illustrated

The carpet is your children's playground. Have them beaten or shampooed by our improved method.

Tradesman's circular

IT MUST BE TRUE

Here is an evening prayer for the little ones, and to me it
is very sweet and solemn:
Saviour, tender Shepherd, hear me,
Bless thy little lamb tonight;
In the darkness be Thou near me,
Keep me safe till morning light.
To remove rust from window glass, dip
cloth in coal oil and rub hard.

Kansas City Star

Undoubtedly the club is the place for a bachelor. It is not
right, however, for a married man to pass the evenings
away from home while his poor wife sadly rocks the cradle
with one foot and wipes away the tears with the other.

Church Sermon

Now Mr. Holland followed the ordinary procedure of having tennis courts on the lawn at the back of his house, from which can be obtained a grand panoramic view towards the Chiltern Hills, which he built for himself 24 years ago.

Oxford Mail

Mrs. Andrews was pleasantly surprised November 25th on her 75th birthday by many expressions of love from her friends. Her daughter, Mrs. Spencer, had a family in her honour.

Chateaugay (N.Y.) Record

Lady desires post; domesticated,
fond of cooking children.

Weekly paper

Q. What does the thread count printed on the label of bed sheets and pillowcases indicate?
A. The massacre of Fort Mickinac in 1763 by Chief Pontiac of the Ottawas.

Columbus (Ohio) Citizen

Germs are so small that there may be as many as one billion, seven hundred million of them in a drop of water.

Mobile Press

IT MUST BE TRUE

VISITORS IS REQUESTED NOT TO THROW COFFEE OR OTHER MATTER INTO THIS BASIN. WHY, ELSE IT STUFFS THE PLACE INCONVENIENT FOR THE OTHER WORLD.

Notice above sink in Italian hotel

Pianos, mangles, lawn-mowers or other musical instruments will be welcome.

Parish magazine

To keep flies from marking electric light globes, smear them with camphorated oil.

Weekly paper

To close these special envelopes, first wet the gum, then insert the tongue into lock and draw until you hear it snap.

Lloyd's bank instructions

I would like your help concerning my receiver which has developed a fault. I find that when I turn up the contrast control to its proper setting, I get a dirty picture.

Practical Television

Aunts in the house are a serious nuisance and are not easily expelled once they have established a kingdom. Perhaps a chemist in your town could help you.

People's Friend

Dripping faucets, sticking doors, rattling windows, faulty light sockets, jammed drawers are among the many things you can learn to make easily and quickly.

Advertiser's circular

However, some 13,500 other American citizens are now playing nursemaid to these South American rodents, envisioning wealth beyond the dreams of Ava Rice.

Pittsburgh Press

Q. How should a card sent to a divorcee be addressed?
A. Address the envelope to Mrs. Jones Smith. Correctly a divorcee drops her ex-husband's first name, and in its place uses her maiden surname (in this case, Robinson).

Newark News

COOK WANTED, MARCH 1ST.
COMFORTABLE ROOM WITH RADIO; TWO
IN FAMILY; ONLY ONE WHO CAN BE WELL
RECOMMENDED.

Ad in Hereford paper

Lady with one child 2½ years seeks situation as housekeeper. oGod cook.

Ad in South African paper

To prevent suffocation, babies should never be allowed to lie face down on their backs, said officials of the Canadian Mothercraft Society.

Canadian paper

TO OPEN JAR, PIERCE WITH A PIN TO
RELEASE VACUUM – THEN PUSH OFF.

Inscription on fruit jar

WANTED–A domesticated lady to live with an elderly lady to hell with the cooking and housework.

Notice in agency window

WOMAN KICKED BY HER HUSBAND SAID TO BE GREATLY IMPROVED

Headline in Illinois paper

My wife took an instant dislike to my guests and went out of her way to make painful scones.

Evening paper

Plastic makes a new space saver for mothers who lives in crowded quarters or who must travel with a small baby in the form of an inflatable bathtub.

Dallas Morning News

Before wearing black woollen stockings stand for 10 minutes in boiling water coloured with washing blue.

Laundry hint in cookery book

Be sure to keep your children away from this poison. This may not kill them at once but gradually they will all die.

Farming paper

WANTED — A GOOD COOK;
KITCHEN-MAID KEPT; SMALL FAIRY.

> Provincial paper

CRIME/LAW
& ORDER

Ghana is to change over to driving on the right. The change will be made gradually.

Ghana paper

POLICE FOUND SAFE UNDER BLANKET

Headline in Gloucestershire Echo

'But we do not want a repetition of the farce that occurred on the last occasion we saw the Board,' he said, 'when a lot of sand was thrown in our eyes. This time we want something more concrete.'

Fulham Chronicle

NOTICE. ANY PERSONS PASSING BEYOND THIS POINT WILL BE DROWNED.

By order of the magistrates
Sign in Essex

Capt. Lindholm and other officers emphasized that women should call police if they are accosted, or if they think they see or hear a prowler.

'We'll be there the next night,' he asserted.

Los Angeles Times

P.C. Roberts said he found the horse straying riding the bicycle. Noticing he was swaying a good deal, and that he had no trouser clips on, witness stopped him and questioned him about the cycle.

Kent paper

Mrs Perkins had pleaded guilty to obtaining and possessing a total of 40 oz. of opium and other drugs (18,000 dozes).

Glasgow paper

She was a pathetic figure as she stood in the box, wearing a blue coat and a dark straw hat, with a spray of artificial trousers.

Liverpool paper

Two private inquiry agents said they had climbed to 20 ft up a popular tree near King's Lynn Flats, Ithaca Road, to watch a bedroom in Mrs C—'s flat one night.

The Sun, Sydney

A large row of pink earls belonging to a well-known lady of noble birth has been restored to her.

South Wales Echo

Before the verdict was rendered this morning 'Miss Mexico' told interviewers that if the court freed her, she would become a nut.

Chicago Daily Tribune

Walleyes Police issued the following description of a man whose body was recovered from the Mersey, near New Brighton, yesterday morning: Age between 30 and 40, 5 ft 9 in. tall, good build, tattoo on left forearm of woman kneeling on a chair holding a fan, wearing dark striped suit, two print shirts, woollen vest, grey socks and black boots.

Evening Express

These thugs must be stopped and I intend to see that they are. Rule 4a in the council rent book says that parents must keep their parents under control.

The Daily Telegraph

To relieve congestion, take Astoria ferry every fifteen minutes.

Ad on Queensboro Bridge, New York

VANCOUVER: DALE MARTIN,
AN ENTERTAINER, HAS BEEN ORDERED
BY A PROVINCIAL COURT JUDGE TO AVOID
MAKING ANYONE PREGNANT FOR THE
NEXT THREE YEARS. THE ORDER NOT TO
IMPREGNATE ANY GIRLS CAME FROM
JUDGE LESLIE BEWLEY, WHO GAVE
MARTIN A SUSPENDED SENTENCE AND
THE THREE-YEAR PROBATION FOR
POSSESSION OF AN OFFENSIVE WEAPON.

Toronto Globe

Her husband said they hadn't really been fighting: 'We were arguing,' he claimed. Each defendant was fined £2. Wedding Bells Place an order for this journal with your newsagent and avoid disappointment.

Holborn and Finsbury Guardian

When police found him with the two girls he said that one was a piece and the other a neighbour.

The Evening News

Evans says putting a man to death eliminates hope of rehabilitation.

Olympia (Wash.) Olympian

David Ernest M— was paid £5 for having no licence for his van and £8 for speeding.

Lancashire Evening Telegraph

As a result of the incident many of the busts leaving Uxbridge Terminus are being followed by police cars.

Local paper

Chief Detective T. G. Jackson told the Court that Smith was employed as a carter, and while taking a load of rubbish away had stolen the varnish. Prior to this there had been no stain against his character.

New Zealand paper

The customs search was continued when the ship arrived at Tilbury – and the half-ounce of drug was found by a specially trained dog hidden in a hosepreel.

Oldham Evening Chronicle

A Grand Jury in Los Angeles have indicted welterweight boxer Art Aragon on a charge of offering a bride to an opponent.

Bradford Telegraph and Argus

It is time the law stepped in to prohibit people who have no more sense than to make their dogs follow them on bicycles, especially at night.

Letter in Leicester Mercury

Alderman Johnston moved that, pending the passing of the street by-law, that all vehicles on Columbia Street be required to keep to the left going up and to the right going down.

The British Columbian

In America it is true that our general rules of evidence and principles of law are mainly followed, and there is very little danger of an innocent man being acquitted.

The Globe

The Nebraska legislature was asked to enact a law providing annulment of marriages of all couples who do not within three years after the wedding have one or more children by Representative Hines, Democrat of Omaha, who is a bachelor.

Radio News aboard U.S.S. Pennsylvania

Sir Hendry D— was presented today with the honorary Freedom of Plymouth. The magistrate remanded him in custody 'in order to get the alcohol out of his system'.

Evening paper

BEWARE!
TO TOUCH THESE WIRES
IS INSTANT DEATH
ANYONE FOUND DOING SO WILL BE
PROSECUTED

Signboard

The man who would stoop so low as to write an anonymous letter, the least he could do would be to sign his name to it.

Letter in Irish paper

The gutted carcase of a deer was found yesterday afternoon near Fonthill Road. While investigating this, State Trooper Howard Johnson was bitten on the left arm by a dog owned by Miss Ann Lacko of Fonthill Road. Police at the local sub-station said the dog would be let loose and Johnson tied up for ten days.

New Jersey paper

THE POLICE ANNOUNCE THAT DOGS WITHOUT DOLLARS FOUND WANDERING AFTER 10 P.M. ARE LIABLE TO BE DESTROYED.

Hong Kong paper

POLICE DISBELIEVE A NAVAL STOKER WHO SAYS HE IS NOT DEAD

Daily paper

Prosecutor Charles Bell asked all the prospective jurors if they would inflict the death penalty 'if the evidence warranted it'. Those who said they were opposed to capital punishment under any circumstances were executed.

Cincinnati Times Star

The van was left unattended by the driver who went into a restaurant for dinner and later was found empty at Holloway.

Provincial paper

```
$25 reward to anyone finding red male
chow dog or to anyone saying they
killed this dog. C. W. Myers, 834 M,
Liberty St., Phone 9267.
```
North Carolina paper

Mr. Firestone argued that his client was a student,
had not been found guilty, and should not be sub-
hauled by tank steamer to the east coast, and then
pumped back into the middle-west and the Great
Lakes area through pipe-lines

Cleveland Press

The Suffragette leader, looking very pale and
emancipated, was driven out of prison in a closed
carriage.

Dublin Saturday Herald

The vendor's solicitor will then send you the daft
agreement and ask you to sign it.

Weekly paper

The word lawyer, he argued, was a
general term, and was not confined to
solicitors, but anybody who practised
any breach of the law.

Cambridge paper

REVOLTING POLICE TAKE OVER BOLIVIA

Iowa paper

On Thursday a large band of rebels wearing uniforms, and fully equipped with rifles and ammunition, concentrated in the village of Kilmanagh, County Kilkenny. They bivouacked for some hours behind a barricade composed of creamery cats.

Provincial paper

During the past few days three bicycles have been stolen from Exeter streets. The police consider that a bicycle thief is at work.

Western Morning News

FALSE CHARGE OF THEFT OF HENS POLICE ON WILD GOOSE CHASE.

Kent paper

By an unfortunate typographical error we were made to say last week that the retiring Mr. —— was a member of the defective branch of the police force. Of course this should have read: 'The detective branch of the police farce.'

New Zealand paper

The lad was described as lazy, and when his mother asked him to go to work he threatened to smash her brains out. The case was adjourned for three weeks in order to give the lad another chance.

Manchester paper

Miss Olive Inglis proved to be a young woman wearing a green costume, and a hat trimmed with yellow lace. As there was a previous conviction for a similar offence, she was ordered to find a surety or undergo twenty-one days imprisonment.

Daily Chronicle

225

NUDIST NABBED UNCLOTHED MAN, WHO ADMITS BRANDISHING PISTOL, IS CHARGED WITH CARRYING CONCEALED WEAPON

Providence Journal

Witness was at the house at about three o'clock on the previous afternoon, and he saw P——- through the window. He rang the bell, and the maid answered the door, but declined to open it, and told him to go to a very warm place. He had been there about four times previously but had not seen P——-.

Southport Guardian

Whether the bear was too strong for the cage, or the cage too weak for the bear, may be a subject for investigation.

Daily Mail

NO PERSON SHALL DISCHARGE OR CAUSE TO BE DISCHARGED ANY FIREARM OR OTHER LETHAL WEAPON ON OR WITHIN SIXTY FEET OF ANY STATE HIGHWAY, EXCEPT WITH INTENT TO DESTROY SOME NOXIOUS ANIMAL, OR AN OFFICER OF THE POLICE IN THE PERFORMANCE OF HIS DUTY.

Ordinance of the State of Nebraska

Presiding Superior Judge R-- G-- will be speaker, and he will tell some humorous anecdotes while doing some underwater spear-fishing.

Santa Ana (California) Register

FROM THE HOURS FIXED FOR MEALS ON NO ACCOUNT WILL BE DEVIATED. FOR DAMAGE TO FURNITURE THE PROPRIETOR WILL AVENGE HIMSELF ON THE PERSON COMMITTING THE SAME.

Notice in hotel at Soerabaja, Java

In conclusion, Sir, I enclose my card and remains,
Yours truly
VICTIM

The Market Mail

Mr. Jackson saw two men acting suspiciously and told Sergeant Harrison. The Sergeant surrounded the building.

Leicester paper

At Taunton this week an ex-soldier was charged on remand with having bigamously married, his awful wife being alive.

West Country paper

Would the person who removed Petticoat from the Railways Fence, between 11th and 12th, kindly return same and save further exposure.

Provincial paper

There is a sub-department of Scotland Yard which looks after Kings and visiting potentates, Cabinet Ministers, spies, anarchists, and other undesirables.

South London paper

Although her mother was in it, thieves stole a suitcase containing jewellery and clothing from the car of Miss Dorothy Sampson yesterday afternoon.

West Country paper

DEVIZES MOTORIST HEAVILY PENALIZED SUSPENDED FROM THE WHEEL FOR A MONTH

Wiltshire Gazetteer

They had to pass through an iron grille and a wooden door. The officer opened the iron grille, and while he was opening the wooden door Jackson made a bolt for it.

The Star

It was not until the outcry after the robbery that the burglars knew they had made such a valuable haul. Then they were faced with the impossibility of selling their plunder.

WHY NOT SELL IT THROUGH A SMALL ADVERTISEMENT IN THE HERALD?

Australian paper

Dr. Daly, discussing the request for an enquiry, said he might make a foul statement later.

Bermuda paper

The new decree increases the French Customs Duties by thirty per cent, expect for newsprint and cellulose used in the manufacture of sausages and certain cheese.

Chinese paper

**RURAL COUNCIL DISTRICT BIRTHRATE
IS HIGHEST FOR TEN YEARS
HUMANE KILLER ADOPTED**

Sussex paper

LOW CONVERSATION ALLOWED

Notice in public gallery

WHEN TWO MOTOR VEHICLES MEET AT AN INTERSECTION, EACH SHALL COME TO A FULL STOP AND NEITHER SHALL PROCEED UNTIL THE OTHER HAS GONE.

New Hampshire traffic regulation

Two cycles belonging to girls that had been left leaning against lamp-posts were badly damaged.

Glasgow paper

Later he said, 'You may go to the devil.' Plaintiff then said he went to his solicitor.

Police Court News

Until further notice, no steam-roller, steam-wagon, heavy lorry, or charabanc, will be allowed to run over the bride.

Bedford paper

The officer in command kept his head and cleverly ordered his men to keep behind it as it moved forward.

Daily paper

P.C. Thomas said he arrested the defendant because his face was beyond the limit fixed for the town.

Manchester paper

Referring to Mr. C. T. Williams, the magistrate said: 'It's not everyone who has the courage to tickle an armed intruder.'

Daily paper

She could not say on which side of the road he was riding in Commissioner Street, but he turned into West Street on the wrong side. She was sure that after the accident she fell on to the pavement on the correct side of the road.

Johannesburg Star

In many other towns the trolley buses are virtually silent. Surely it is not beyond the ingenuity and industry of Birmingham to stop the awful screech ours make as the conductor runs along the overhead wire.

Letter in the Birmingham Mail

The will disposes of a million-dollar estate, the bunk going to relatives.

Washington Star

Information wanted as to the
whereabouts of Mrs. J. O. Plonk
(Blonk) wife of J. O. Plonk (Clonk).

Ad in Chinese paper

PARISIAN BEHEADED
FOR KILLING
WIFE BEFORE MISTRESS

St. Louis Post-Dispatch

*The best thing to do with people who write
anonymous letters is to put them straight in
the fire.*

Letter in Provincial paper

CHILDREN FOUND STRAYING WILL BE
TAKEN TO THE LION HOUSE.

Notice in Zoo

UNNATURAL/
NATURAL
DISASTERS

DON'T THROW PEOPLE BELOW.
>Notice on Southend pier

A gale attaining a velocity of 72 miles an hour swept over New York last night. Humorous persons were injured by falling signs and bricks.
>West Indian paper

The accident occurred on the bend of No. 16 platform while the driver of the stationary train was taking gin water.
>Manchester paper

Motor vehicle safety belts must be installed rigidly enough to withstand a sudden thirst.
>Trenton Times

It is proposed to re-align the road to cut out a dangerous double bed which has been the scene of numerous serious accidents in recent years.
>Oxford Times

It appears that a slippery quality in a road surface is caused by the use of tar, or of bitumen, and that the condition can be avoided by the use of bitumen, or of tar.
>Lincolnshire paper

Efforts to rescue three cows trapped halfway down 500-ft cliffs on the Dorset coast, near Lulworth, have been called off. A Defence Ministry statement said that they would be replaced by younger men.

West Lancashire Evening Gazette

IN CASE OF FIRE, PLEASE DO YOUR
UTMOST TO ALARM THE HALL PORTER

Notice in Austrian hotel

The dangers of the Taupo-Napier road were also brought home to us as it was on the metalled part of this road that we saw the only two accidents during our tour. One was the over-turned petrol tanker blazing away with the hillsides in flames around it. The other was a saloon car carrying women and children upside down at the side of the road.

Napier (NZ) Daily Telegraph

Mr F— sustained severe bruising, his wife had three stitches inserted in a forehead laceration. Julie had a fractured collarbone and Gary facial bruises, which caused rejoicing.

Pocklington Times

A 17-year-old boy died in the New Plymouth hospital as a result of injuries received in a car crash at Inglewood. He was Rex Manton, who died less than two hours after the accident. His condition was reported tonight to be satisfactory.

> Hamilton Times, New Zealand

Donald's father told the court that his son's personality had completely changed since the accident. His career in the catering industry was finished because of the accident and he still carried a chip on his shoulder.

> Kentish Gazette

The speaker told of his adventure with a perilous bra constrictor.

> Methodist newsletter

OWING TO THE DISASTROUS FIRE, THE GRANGE HOTEL HAS TEMPORARILY MOVED TO GREYFIELDS MANOR HOTEL, WHERE THE WELCOME WILL BE EVEN WARMER.

> Ad in ABC railway timetable

Discovered at 5.06 a.m. the flames starting on the third floor of the Midwest Salvage Co., spread so rapidly that the first firemen on the scene were driven back to safety and leaped across three streets to ignite other buildings.

Cincinnati Times Star

Freaks of the cold spell
... The harbour and long Island Sound were covered thick with ice and a large number of transatlantic steamers could not get in. Traffic was almost at a standstill. In a village near New York a woman was found in bed beside her husband.

Neue Wurzbürge Zeitung

There was no damage to the truck, but the two front fenders, headlights, bumper-guard, and girl of Fitzgerald's car were damaged.

Mamaroneck (New York) Times

In a collision of autos on Sylvan Street, a Ford sedan sustained a cut of the nose and bruise on the leg but declined medical aid.

Malden (Mass.) Evening News

I phoned for the N.F.S. and they were here in three minutes. They did a wonderful job. The first and second floors are gutted, and the shop is a shambles.

Weymouth Southern Times

When approaching roadways are wider than bridges, the accident rate is only about one eighth, or less, than when the bridge is narrower than the approach.

Los Angeles paper

Cross-channel steamers from Liverpool, Heysham, and Glasgow made Belfast three hours late. One of these brought down the committee tent at Shrewsbury Hospital races after police and others had rescued the takings just in time.

Daily paper

Besides school-children, motorists are often compelled in springtime to include frogs and toads among their objects of compulsory nature study; because you cannot help noticing some of the things which you kill.

Motoring journal

Confused by the noise of traffic, a cow that probably was experiencing its first taste of city life, got mixed up with vehicles in Milwaukee Avenue yesterday and was struck by a street car. It was so badly injured that Patrolman Stegmiller ended its life with a bullet.

Detroit News

The Fire Brigade was soon on the scene, and once they commenced to turn their noses on to the flames the conflagration was soon under control.

Egyptian Mail

A big music store in the centre of Louisville has been completely burned out. The brigade played on the burning instruments for many hours.

Northern Daily Mail

London firemen with rescue gear were called early today to Dorset Street, Marylebone, when a man fell into a basement yard. He was lifted to road level, injured, and taken to hospital.

Daily Mail

KEEP SUPPLIES OF WATER AND SAND AVAILABLE, ESPECIALLY IN UPPER STORIES AND ROOMS AT THE BOTTOM OF WELLS.

Civil Defence Leaflet

STEAMER COLLIDES IN FOG

The Norwegian steamer Gaea, put into dock at Dover today with her bows damaged as the result of a collision with an unknown Football at Woolwich and Fulham

Pall Mall Gazette

On entering the Hiratsura tunnel something went wrong with the locomotive, the train coming to a standstill and remaining in the tunnel some time. Finally the driver managed to get the train into motion, when it was found that one of the drivers was missing. A search was made and the driver was discovered lying unconscious in the funnel.

Peking Times

Heavy rains again feel in Khartoum and vicinity last Saturday night and several lakes have been formed in various parts of the town, some of which are still navigable. Mosquitos are not allowed to breed in them, under the penalty of a heavy fine.

Egyptian Mail

The cause of the explosion is unknown, but it is assumed that some combustible matter was among the coal.

Dorset paper

The driver had a narrow escape, as a broken board penetrated his cabin and just missed his head. This had to be removed before he could be released.

Leicester paper

The machine landed at Croydon safety and no one was hurt. One of the passengers had his trousers singed. The damage was confined to the undercarriage, where a tear was found in the fabric.

News Chronicle

It is estimated that a quarter of a million sterling's worth of damage was done in the Butler's Bridge Wharf fire. The firemen are still playing horses on the smouldering debris.

Malta paper

WOMAN HURT WHILE COOKING HER HUSBAND'S BREAKFAST IN A HORRIBLE MANNER.

Headline in Texas paper

All the six main workships were destroyed, five of them severely.

Daily paper

Jenkins, it is claimed, was driving at a high rate of speed and swerving from side to side. As he approached the crossing he started directly towards it and crashed into Miss Miller's rear end which was sticking out into the road about a foot. Luckily she escaped injury and the damage can easily be remedied with a new coat of paint.

Ohio paper

A full charge of shot struck Mr. Cozad squarely in the back door of the henhouse.

Illinois paper

Policeman Leo Grant was shot through the stomach and John Marcinoak, taxi-cab driver, through the hip, while a trusty at the jail was shot in the excitement.

San Francisco call-bulletin

Mrs. Lukes was caught beneath the auto and taken to St. Joseph's Hospital with several fractured bones. The bones were on their way to Woonsocket to spend their holiday.

Connecticut paper

One of these men, a Calabrian named Motta, went to his partner's shop and tried to shoot him while he was engaged in shaving a customer. The bullet shaved the face of a boy who was waiting.

Egyptian Gazette

The Brigade was called and distinguished the flames.

Evening paper

The Lomas Fire Brigade was soon on the scene and helped by members of the railway personnel were able to reduce the two carriages to a smouldering heap.

Buenos Aires Herald

The fire, which started at 8.30 a.m., was extinguished after six hours fight. It was thought that combustion was the cause of the fire.

Illinois paper

The motorist stuck miles from anywhere has only himself to blame if he has not brought an up-to-date road mop.

Weekly Pictorial

Mrs. Alice McCrory and son, Harvey, went to Dayton last Sunday to visit Mr. and Mrs. Carl Dunbar, who were slightly injured in an automobile accident last week. Mrs. Dunbar before her accident was Miss Olivia McCrory.

Ohio paper

HOBBIES

Conceived in the summer of 1959, the
38-year-old Managing Director J. G.
Robinson (known in the motoring world
as Jeff) has watched this model
develop after being thoroughly tested
in the Welsh mountains.

Ad in The Queen

From Llandrindod you proceed along the lovely
valley of the Ithon, growing more beautiful as you
proceed.

Motor Cycle

James Ward, R.A., gained the prize, but being too
large to hang his painting was rolled up and placed
in Chelsea Hospital

Trade publication

The first swallow has arrived at Devizes. It was spotted by
Police Constable John Cooke of Seend, whose hobby is
bird-watching, sitting wet and bedraggled on telephone
wires at the Prison Bridge, Devizes, on Sunday.

Western Gazette

Arthur already holds black belt grades in Judo and Karate,
so this award makes him a leading marital arts practitioner
in the Isle of Man.

Mona's Herald

One night he heard noises from the terrace, and investigated, fearing mischief, but found that the noises were being made by members of the astronomical society studying plants through their telescopes.

Mid-Sussex Times

I oiled up the cylinders well before cranking, and also checked over the ignition system well, including a spirited performance of 'We came from the mountains' by Bach, and the sparking plugs. What do you think causes the engine to run unevenly?

Query in motoring paper

Then in another London hotel there is Mr. Johnson, the Manager, who has studied pigs all his life.

Canadian paper

While your partner is dealing the cards you should be snuffling.

Daily paper

At about one o'clock when the eclipse was on the sun, I saw a most beautiful star shining very bright, and I pointed this out to three ladies who were watching the eclipse in a bath of water. Is this an unusual occurrence?

Letter in West London paper

A PRETTY KNITTING PATTERN
Cast on any to serve: – To each pound of carrot pulp
number of stitches that can be divided by five; 1st row
Knit 1.

Northampton Daily Chronicle

Most of the owner-drivers I know make a practice
of washing their ears at least once a week.

Motoring paper

*My reference to gargoyles – and I am still
without any explanation of the ones anciently
in Eastgate – reminds me that I recently had
a lady from the Norton area call to see me.*

Gloucester Citizen

FICTIONAL
STORIES

'Why are you here today, Mr . . . . . Lomax?' Alice stumbled over the unfamiliar name. Mark reached out his hand to help her to her feet.

Woman's World

```
I felt my hair being yanked cruelly as
I tumbled to the ground. Audrey's
hate-crazed face hoovered over me.
```
Modern Confessions

Cooler in the South, Warmer in the South is the seven-day forecast of the *Sunday Express* weather experts.

Sunday Express

Horace picked up a shabby-looking volume. His ear, keen for an approaching footstep, turned over the leaves.

Guernsey paper

He went across to the fireplace and stood with his back to its warmth, staring into the fire with unseeing eyes.

Short story

Marjorie would often take her eyes from the deck and cast them far out to sea.

Short story

He had killed Nana once and she had ignored it. Too inexperienced perhaps to make anything of it.

Dallas Times-Herald

Among the first to enter was Mrs. Clara Adams of Erie, lone woman passenger. Slowly her nose was turned away from the hangar doors to face in a south-westerly direction. Then like some strange beast she crawled along the grass.

Burbank (California) Post

The half-starving man sat down at the rough deal table and began to eat it ravenously.

Sunday paper serial

McVeigh hesitated. His eyes flickered over Reilly's face, dropped to the floor, went back to the papers. He picked them up, arranged them nearly, laid them down carefully.

Magazine story

He stopped and re-lit his cigarette with a great light in his eyes.

Scottish paper

Send mother a gift of hardly ever blooming rose bushes.

Sioux Falls Argus Leader

On the other hand, a lady in a thin black dress and widow's veil, turned away and with a curling lip began to turn over a book lying on a table near her.

From a novel

'Mr. Perkins might be able to help you,' she said, as she took down a dusty lodger from the shelf.

Weekly magazine

They had hardly got into the skipper's cabin when a tremendous pitch on the steamer sent Leila rolling on the floor. Before she could be got under control again she had shipped hundreds of tons of water. Then her nose went down and her tail went up and for a moment it was a question if she right herself. A wriggle and a roll and she saved herself.

From a novel

He returned in a few minutes and announced the visitor in faultless English - 'Signor Tillizini'.

Short story

Bob guided her to the spinet. He took his spectacles off his beaky nose and invited Mrs. Ransome to admire it.
'It's much smaller than Aunt Bertha's,' she said.

Modern Woman

She stood at the foot of the stairs, narrowing her eyes and breathing through her hips.

Saturday Evening Post

He sat there quite calmly, a pipe wedged between his lids.

Boys' paper

Joe lifted his eyes quietly a moment to hers then sat down to his coffee. Without opening his mouth again, he finished this, hesitated, arose . . .

Story in American magazine

The eminent statistician rubbed his ear thoughtfully and produced a cigarette.

Short story

There were two sharp retorts, and Radley lunched and staggered.

Short story

Erwen was a man of keen observation. There was something in his visitor's eyes which puzzled him. Suddenly he realized what it was. It was the whisky and soda which he had set down untasted at the corner of the table.

From a serial by E. Phillips Oppenheim

'If you ask me,' said Doris, 'it's more like twelve years they have been married. I don't think they will ever have a chill now.'

Short story

She proceeded on her way until 7, or rather later, when a noise was heard as of a heavy body like an anchor or a chain being dragged along the deck from about the funnel aft. It was the mate's watch.

Liverpool paper

The faces of the two men were livid with rage as she quietly crumpled them up and threw them on the fire.

Short story

It was one of those perfect June nights that so seldom occur except in August.

Magazine story

The skipper spat disconsolately down the engine-room ventilator and stopped the engines.

Sea story

Lady wishes to travel in exquisite lingerie.

Daily paper

They looked out of the window as the train drew into Crewe station. 'Hull!' they cried, 'we're there.'

Short story

LOOKS

To emphasise the shape of the eyes, pencil in a fine brown line actually following the growth of the lashes. Mascara must be made into a nice creamy consistency and lower lashes made up well with lemon curd and ice the top with lemon water icing, or sprinkle icing sugar on top.

Greenock Telegraph

Princess Margaret's daring but very fashionable hat caused a sensation when she opened a school for the blind at Sevenoaks.

France-Soir

This woman walked very close to me, and it was obvious that underneath her clothing she wore little or nothing.

The Sun

Her dark hair is attractively set, and she has fine fair skin, which, she admits ruefully, comes out 'in a mass of freckles' at the first hint of sin.

Essex County Standard

He looked almost square, as if his tailor had put too much pudding in the shoulders.

Toronto Star

Miss Sandiston, who is only 19, has grown since last year. In patches her form is most impressive.

Essex paper

Like Adela, he had dark brown hair, with enormous black eyebrows, a moustache, and a short beard.
From 'A marriage of inconvenience' by Thomas Cobb

'Heavens, I am thirty!' she said. 'Please get me a drink.'
Magazine story

The large spectacles that he wore halfway down his hooked nose did not disguise the fact that the latter were red with weeping.
Daily Mail

This Appliance will reduce your
Hips, or Bust
Ad in People's Home Journal

One of the first to arrive at the church was Lady D—, nearly attired in a dove-grey costume.
Bedford paper

Princess B— wore a white and gold lace gown which she'd saved for the occasion. To give you an idea how elaborate it was, the centre-piece was a mirror 13½ feet long with elaborate matching candelabra of fruit-baskets.
Los Angeles Mirror

Baldness starts when the rate of hair fall exceeds the rate of replacement.

> American Buying Guide

Nylon lace panties are among the new examples of nylon lingerie.
Lord Hailsham also wore a soft silk shirt.

> Northern Daily Mail

It's a good idea, before you give your hair its nightly brushing, to begin the operation with a brick massage to loosen your scalp and to start the circulation of the blood.

> Ann Arbor (Michigan) News

The new spring styles are so varied that no one can fail to obtain a hat that will not suit them.

> Rochdale Observer

Can you advise me what to do with my face? I've had it for several years and it seems to get no better.

> Women's paper

What is more beautiful for the blonde to wear for formal dances than white tulle? My answer – and I'm sure you will agree with me – is 'Nothing'.

Worcester (Massachusetts) Evening Gazette

Today's hint tells you how to keep your hair in first-class order. Cut it out and paste it on a piece of cardboard and hang it in your bathroom.

Essex paper

Fashion says that bikinis are out, and full-length swim suits are in. But British beach girls are revolting.

The People

You really have seen only half the show if you see the Paris imports worn on the mannequins alone. There is almost double the excitement in looking under and inside the clothes.

Women's Wear Daily

Tibetans in no way resemble the neighbouring Chinese but are quite like the Americans. They are big, truculent men who live simply and practise polyandry, four or five men taking one wife.

American paper

Convection currents in the underlying rocks provide the energy and mechanical requirements needed to make possible the gradual drift or motion of woman's pale green two-piece suit on April 17th.

West Country paper

Even without his beautifully tailored clothes he was the sort of man people looked at twice, especially women.

From 'The Lady is Afraid' by G. H. Coxe

If your skin is not liable to be sensitive, rub the arms gently with pumice stone. This will take them right off.

Woman's paper

MISCELLANEOUS

Sagittarius (Nov 22 – Dec 22). Precautions should be taken against running into unforeseen occurrences or events.

New Chronicle

Catherine had always been lucky. Even the sun was shining when she first saw it.

Short story

As soon as Miss W— knew she was to sin, she telephoned her husband in Kansas.

New York Times

A tough age, yes. Uncomfortable, risky, expensive. But also the most glorious and exciting age the race has ever known. Never have humans beings reached so far toward the stars, dared dig so deep in the mire.

I'm glad to be living in this day! Thank God for its constant change and challenge and give me the courage to keep in line.

The halibut always lies on its left side, which is practically white, and both eyes and the colouration are on the right side.

Trenton (New Jersey) Times

Our photograph shows a typical Poole street scene, though actually it was taken in Lymington last summer.

West Country paper

Speed of drying of wood is primarily dependent upon the rate of removal of moisture from the timber.

Manchester Guardian Commercial

Will the person who was nosey enough to write me that letter which was none of their business and who knew nothing about it please be man enough to admit it.

Announcement in Pennsylvania paper

Henry VIII by his own efforts increased the population of England by 40,000.

Northern San Diego Shopper's Guide

The coat of arms includes, as Supporters, a man and woman, representing Adam and Eve, wreathed round the waist with leaves, all proper.

Weekly Illustrated

Lamps must be long enough to be efficient, and the average length is likely to increase. Prolonged deliberation at one laboratory has produced the following rule on maximum lamp length: 'No lamp shall be longer than the maximum dimension of the room it is intended to fit.'

Electrical Engineering

Nobody ever shouted 'Good old Albert' to the bearded husband of Victoria, but plenty of people have shouted it to the easy-going debonair Philip.

Associated Press